LIMINAL
CONSCIOUSNESS

LIMINAL CONSCIOUSNESS

Developing Leaders, Teams, and Organizations for a Better World

Edwin E. Olson

First published in 2023 by the NTL Institute
NTL Institute is an imprint of Libri Publishing

Copyright © Edwin E. Olson

The right of Edwin E. Olson to be identified as the author of this work has been asserted in accordance with the Copyright, Designs and Patents Act, 1988.

The author is a member of NTL Institute for Applied Behavioral Science. Views expressed are those of the author alone.

ISBN: 978-1-911451-19-8

All rights reserved.

A CIP catalogue record for this book is available from The British Library

Cover design by Amy Hadden

Libri Publishing
Brunel House
Volunteer Way
Faringdon
Oxfordshire
SN7 7YR

Tel: +44 (0)845 873 3837

www.libripublishing.co.uk

Praise for Liminal Consciousness: Developing Leaders, Teams, and Organizations for a Better World

Einstein said we can't solve problems using the same mindset that created them. True but infuriating: for how can one mindset choose to surrender to another? This is the question Edwin Olson answers in his new book, *Liminal Consciousness: Developing Leaders, Teams, and Organizations for a Better World.* If you conclude this book with the same mindset with which you began it, you'll have your answer, and humanity is doomed. Maybe read it a second time.

— RABBI RAMI SHAPIRO, author of *Holy Rascals* and *The World Wisdom Bible*

Liminal Consciousness: Developing Leaders, Teams, and Organizations for a Better World by Edwin Olson provides an essential exploration and roadmap for how to source and apply our Consciousness-given potentials for co-creating thrivable worlds and futures. This inspirational guidebook will radically shift, as well as deepen and expand, your understanding of Consciousness as fundamental reality. As Olson points out, in order to reach a tipping point for effectively addressing our systemic global crisis, it is essential that we do so from a Consciousness worldview. Only then can we transform the root causes of the worsening sustainability crisis, which reflects our own crisis in consciousness. *Liminal Consciousness* is a must-read for anyone who is serious about the necessary inner and outer changes for our world in transformation. Discover how you can align yourself, and your work, with the fundamental unity and wholeness of life and existence, through values that can heal our divided worlds, and based on wisdom that evolves our human consciousness.

– ANNELOES SMITSMAN, PhD, LLM, co-author of the *Future Humans Trilogy,* founder & CEO of EARTHwise Centre

I have had my business head on all my life. Towards the end of my business career, I found it harder and harder to focus on business. I then found myself being pulled more and more into the spiritual world and getting my spiritual head on. That lead me into a whole new world that I never knew existed. Ed's book was a reality check for me that confirms the need to instill consciousness with business. I only wish that I had been able to migrate these two things earlier in my life and hope you will be able to do this for yourself. Since there is a movement in the business world towards meditation and consciousness, the need for Ed's Worldwide Consciousness is now.

– TOM COCKLEY, retired CEO, business owner, Gulden Ophthalmics

This is a timely book, accentuating our collective need to transcend our tight sense of ego-identity and adversarial tendencies by opening to the greater all-pervading Consciousness that connects and supports all life. Opening to this greater, universal setting of Consciousness, subtly connects us with the intelligent Source of Love that has brought forth the universe and allows us to tap into and trust the intuitive wisdom that is accessed through this more expanded awareness and broadened, interconnected sense of self. Olson's book also shows how the process can go beyond the mere individual level to the corporate and communal level, which is so vital in addressing the pressing concerns of our current global situation. This is recommended reading!

– GREGORY BLANN, author of *Living Open Space* and *Garden of Mystic Love*

An incredible contribution, extremely compelling and engaging.

– NICOLYA CHRISTI, author of *Love, God & Everything*

This book is going to put the vital aspect of liminality and liminal consciousness in the forefront of people's thinking process. It opens up the mind and nudges gently to think beyond and think differently. The subject of liminal consciousness is very close to Indian culture where existence of the non-existent, invisible power and destiny is given lots of value. I loved the elucidation around the worldview incorporating the consciousness of the liminal space. It's really the need of the hour in these materialistic complex work systems and social systems where people are losing the power of being human which is the epitome of liminality. In the artificial-intelligence-driven world, the tendency is towards materialism and data, but on the contrary, society actually needs those touchpoints of consciousness of the next order. The need to strengthen communication, relationships, understanding and responses depend upon the increased self-awareness that can only come by a process of recognition of the invisible power within. The book creates a much-needed resource guide for a whole system process of inner re-engineering that will create a deep impact on leaders, teams and the better world as the title of the book intends.

– PRAKASH RANJAN, PhD Head of HR for South Asia, Veolia Water Technologies & Solutions

Having read several of Dr. Olson's previous books, I believe he has achieved a synthesis and at a high level of Consciousness for application and action. Why he wrote it and the message behind/in front of it is crystal clear. The theme of each chapter knitted together the tension between the non-material non-dual world of Consciousness and the material dualistic world in which we live and work. Throughout, I resonated with the spirit, intuition and dreams (a la Jung). It represented to me a literature review in the field/area of Consciousness. By following the footnotes, I learned broadly and deeply. Dr. Olson is public with his own learning and discoveries and generous with his sharing in this marvelous 2023 manuscript.

> – ARGENTINE S. CRAIG, PhD, professor, Fielding Graduate University (retired)

I experienced *Liminal Consciousness: Developing Leaders, Teams, and Organizations for a Better World* as a spirit-lifting and hopeful description of how we are learning to liberate "the better angels of our nature" to make this old world a better place for us all. The notion of Hamlet's quote comes to mind: "There are more things in heaven and earth, Horatio, than are dreamt of in your philosophy." While reading I had the sense that Ed was right there with me. I loved the pre and post "Consciousness Assessments" as a way to become engaged. While the book embraces spirituality, Ed is clear that it is not a theological perspective in the traditional sense. Reading the book encouraged me to finish my "Memories and Reflections of a Conflict Resolution Practitioner." On a personal note, as a "cradle Catholic" who is still wary of the concept of "a mindful responsive universe," I am comfortably on board with the notion that "reality is infinite, without form or boundary" and the book's message: "Come on in – The water's fine!"

> – THOMAS O'NEILL DUNNE, professional member of the Alliance for Peacebuilding and co-founder of the U.S.-Muslim Engagement Project. Tom, a former U.S. Navy SEAL officer, led a team of U.S. and Vietnamese war veterans that planted a "peace forest" in a former minefield in Vietnam.

Don't be afraid of this book. Ed Olson is saying one vital thing: we know more than we think we know. Trust our sixth sense that there is more to reality than we can prove, and act accordingly. This single idea opens us to humility, curiosity and hope – the very qualities that sweeten life and enable survival.

> – HARRY HUTSON, PhD, co-author of *Navigating an Organizational Crisis* and *Putting Hope to Work*

I am deeply moved by what I would characterize as a monumental contribution to the theory and practice of consciousness-based transformation. In the armamentarium of practices that seek to transform the consciousness of organizations, there is an urgent need for an approach that is conceptually rigorous, practically robust, metaphysically profound and capable of stimulating the imagination of practitioners and scholars alike. There is also a need to articulate methods and frameworks that can appeal to the pragmatic orientation of leaders while simultaneously stimulating their appetite for an exalted contribution.

The richness of the book is reflective of the author's multidimensionality arising from his fluency in multiple epistemologies, decades of immersion in organizational development work, and a multidisciplinary background that includes philosophy, theology, business, organizational behavior, information technology and political science, to name only a few. The pre-test/post-test instrument that Dr. Olson provides to help the reader assess the impact of the book is a testimony to Dr. Olson's pedagogic versatility in taking a potentially abstract metaphysical topic like liminal consciousness, making it refreshingly accessible while also providing the reader with a user-friendly psychometric guidepost to navigate a complex terrain.

Consciousness, as we all know, is a vast, limitless topic which allows no boundaries. Its branches reach upward to the sky while its roots go deep into the earth. Dr. Olson's book perfectly embodies this duality of taking us to the very heights of human consciousness while also anchoring us firmly in the soil of a shared, holistic soil of oneness.

PARAM SRIKANTIA, Ph.D., professor, Carmel Boyer School of Business, Baldwin-Wallace University, Berea, Ohio

PREVIOUS BOOKS BY

EDWIN E. OLSON

Facilitating Organization Change: Lessons from Complexity Science. San Francisco, CA: Jossey-Bass/Wiley, 2001 (with Glenda H. Eoyang).

Keep the Bathwater: Emergence of the Sacred in Science and Religion. Estero, FL: Island Sound Press, 2009. Available from author.

Finding Reality: Four Ways of Knowing. Bloomington, IN: Archway Publications, 2014.

And God Created Wholeness: A Spirituality of Catholicity. Maryknoll, NY: Orbis Books, 2018. (Received the First Place Award in Faith and Science in 2019 from the Catholic Press Association in the United States and Canada.)

Become Conscious of Wholeness: Humanity's Only Future. Eugene, OR: Resource Publications (an imprint of Wipf & Stock Publishers), 2021.

Contents

Foreword by Dianne Collins	xv
Consciousness Assessment	xxv
Preface: Memo to Organization Leaders and Consultants	xxix
Introduction: A Consciousness Worldview	xxxiii
Part I – Developing Liminal Consciousness	**1**
1 – The Reality of Consciousness	3
2 – Experiencing Betwixt and Between	11
3 – Actions of the Liminal Self	23
Part II – Transforming Our Complex Systems	**33**
4 – Leadership	35
5 – Teams	43
6 – Organizations	53
Part III – Making the World a Better Place	**65**
7 – Liminal Methods for Change	67
8 – Transcend Differences	81
9 – Create Greater Wholes	89
Conclusion: Evolving the Future	105

Repeat Consciousness Assessment	113
Afterword	115
Glossary	117
Appendix – Is Artificial Intelligence Sentient?	125
Select Bibliography	129
Index	137
Acknowledgements	143
About the Author	145

List of Illustrations

Cover	The Liminal Between Materialism and Consciousness	
Figure 1.1 – The Hidden Dimensions of Consciousness		6
Figure 1.2 – Prism Metaphor for Dispersion of Consciousness		7
Figure 2.1 – Formation of Liminal Consciousness		12
Figure 3.1 – As Above, So Below		28
Table 3.1 – Interactions of Two Persons		30
Table 5.1 – Comparison of a "Dream Team" and a Liminal Team		50

Foreword

In times of monumental transformation such as these surrounding us now, we experience a transitional phase where important questions are raised. The questions have no cut-and-dry immediate answers. The lens through which we seek to establish such answers to current and future issues arising as a result of the natural, albeit often tumultuous, evolutionary unfolding of society is of vital significance. Every conversation has content and context that shapes how it's heard. And that is beautiful. From a quantum worldview, there are no fixed and static realities. Gurus and poets, scientists and saints concur: the world is as we see it. Let's take this one leap forward. For awakened thinkers, *the world is as we create it.*

As destiny would have it, Edwin Olson's book *Liminal Consciousness* ironically, serendipitously, and perhaps deliberately comes at this "liminal moment" for humankind. A new state of being for humanity in the throes of awakening toward enlightenment.

"Enlightenment" sounds like a big lofty word not often associated with ordinary daily life and in particular not characteristic of leadership and business organizations. And yet, enlightened leadership may be precisely what is needed more than ever before.

We find ourselves on the precipice of a great shift of societal systems and structures. With converging forces of technologies advancing at superluminal speed it feels as if we are being nudged and even shoved off our reliably familiar platforms and into an abyss of the unknown.

Everyone living in our current era realizes we need new thinking to make the leap across the abyss to a better world. And yet, even as the stuff of science fiction comes to life – artificial generative intelligence (AGI), autonomous vehicles, life-like robots, civilian space travel, bio-cellular healing bots – it is our sacred task to remain true to our human inheritance, the mandate to develop our highest nature utilizing our benefic powers wisely.

If you could think from a new perspective that would change the world, definitively solve our long-standing problems and personal issues as well, what would that perspective be?

A seminal answer to this most pressing issue of our time is ingeniously woven and revealed throughout this book. It offers an opportunity to stretch beyond outdated boundaries to think newly with keen discernment. Reading Edwin's words, you cannot help but be struck by his purpose and dedication to bring forth pivotal knowledge in his comprehensive and finely researched vision and experience. We recognize him as scholar, professor, organizational development expert, seeker of spiritual and scientific wisdom – and most of all as a heartful, soul-conscious, passionate town crier for the good of humanity.

The question that looms large is always, *how?* How does it happen?

To accomplish this requires new understandings. We must understand the true nature of mind as the individualized form of the all-pervasive Consciousness and its inherent creation dynamics. We must have knowledge of the epic paradigm shift in physics from the five-sensory, one-dimensional reality of scientific materialism to the non-material multidimensional reality of quantum mechanics and its implications. We must realize that the pathway "there" is paradoxically not a path, but rather a jump to a new worldview.

To distinguish this further, Edwin had read a blog of mine, "You Can't Get 'There' from 'Here' – Why Change Doesn't Work" based in the QuantumThink® distinction, transformation as distinct from change. It was addressed to business leaders who were stymied by "change" initiatives that didn't seem to be working. When we attempt to eliminate what we don't want by trying to change it, we unwittingly keep that very situation in place. In order to change something, it must be present. "Transformation" means to go beyond the current form. It is a transcendence.

Though Edwin and I have not yet met in person, we share much in common in our respective work and an inner knowing that connects us at a deep level.

We both recognize the vital necessity to glean the implications of the new worldview in physics that has turned topsy-turvy our view of reality from a matter-based to a mind-based world. Where scientists had envisioned the universe to be like a giant machine reducible to its constituent parts, they now view the universe as a giant mind, an unbounded intelligent field of energy in flux which you and I are not separate from, but part and parcel of.

The classical science model (also known as scientific materialism) that spawned the Industrial Age oriented us to know reality through our physical five senses where we "believe" only what we can see, hear, touch, taste, and smell. There's nothing wrong with it per se. We evolved because of it. It gave us much genius. We learned the cause-and-effect dynamic and how to categorize and organize life. We learned to think analytically and became adept at ordinary rational logic. However, it has also kept us limited.

What I lovingly call the *old worldview* locked us into a one-dimensional "only physical matter is real" reality of fixed and solid objects – a machine-like universe separated into parts, chronological time, linear step-by-step logic, and fixed conclusions based in existing circumstances.

The updated and more accurate quantum worldview shows us we live in a much richer experience. It whisks us from the limits of the divisive either/or habit of mind to the ever-expansive realm of both/

and thinking. We live in the interconnectedness of whole systems, of multidimensions extending us beyond the physical, aware of our real superpowers – natural faculties of mind that function in liminal consciousness as intent, intuition, subtle energy, resonance, and meditation. We think from whole systems and expect quantum leaps. It is a view of reality as consciousness-based, unified in its diversity, with infinite possibility as the gift that keeps on giving.

The yearning to relate to reality in a whole other way is something I can honestly say I have spent my lifetime on. To paraphrase the classic genius of the British–American duo comedy act Laurel and Hardie, I wondered how we would ever get ourselves out of this "fine mess." I wanted to discover how we really create a life we love. How can we become masters at co-creating our world in the magnificence we know it can and should be?

My quest to discover a real solution led me to create QuantumThink®. I had the revelation that though we imagine we think freely and independently, actually we don't. Our thinking takes place as a system conditioned by the beliefs, assumptions, and notions derived from our prevailing worldview. As noted, our worldview is essentially what we believe to be true about the nature of reality and how it works, what's possible and what's not.

The quantum worldview is merging with universal wisdom common to all mastery traditions. This new worldview is at the foundation of Edwin's work in distinguishing liminal consciousness. It is also at the foundation of my work in creating QuantumThink®.

At that time, I spoke the words, *we are in a time of evolution unlike any we have witnessed or known when what must evolve now is human consciousness itself.* For me, it is now, and has always been, about awakening to our higher state.

In the past 100 years, our understanding of the nature of reality has indeed undergone a dramatic no-turning-back shift; however, *we* haven't. We're in a Quantum Age yet our thinking is still very much under the influence of Industrial Age worldview assumptions and conclusions, many of which have been shown to be erroneous or limited at best.

Since mind wasn't part of the materialist worldview, we can understand why the natural faculties of mind and Consciousness have yet to become standard curriculum in conventional education. With mind left out of the reality equation, it's clear why the magnitude of liminal consciousness has eluded us.

When you examine the very different characteristics of scientific materialism and quantum principles, you can imagine that truly it's time for a literal quantum leap in consciousness. Think of it this way. Since mind, as the individualized expression of the all-pervasive Consciousness, is the source of what we manifest in the outer world, the most significant shift any of us can have is to awaken our connection to mind. This occurs in liminal consciousness.

The discovery that mind, and not matter as once believed, is fundamental has the power to alter the world. In fact, it already has. The new worldview that Edwin refers to as the consciousness worldview made possible all of our non-linear digital technology from silicon chips and sensors to AR (augmented reality), AI (artificial intelligence), the metaverse, and beyond.

We have been brought together in a virtual way through the Internet, though by all appearances we haven't reached that oneness in our collective heart and soul, mind and spirit. This is our wondrous adventure: to connect our inner ethereal experiences with our outer world manifestations. It happens in liminal consciousness.

Though the new consciousness worldview, which paradoxically has roots in our ancient past as well as in our modern present, has been emerging for nearly 100 years and has been written about prodigiously, it has not yet become mainstream. Edwin Olson and I share the vision and commitment to it being so. It makes sense of so many things that have been conundrums for us.

The tendencies to retreat to our own corners, maintaining silos in business culture, and at odds with one another's subjective credos and ideologies – could these simply be outcomes of separation thinking conditioned in our social fabric from the assumptions, beliefs, and notions of scientific materialism that have embedded themselves in the way we relate to one another?

Leaders, pundits, parents, and politicians wonder whether there is a solution to ending the bitter divisiveness and finally bring about a world of peace, harmony, and joy that is our divine birthright. Often people tend to "blame" the ills of society on "bad people," or the tendency toward authoritarian rule, power-grabbing egotism, or mercenary greed. Yet, consider that these behaviors are actually *effects* of the underlying cause of so many of our problems. We have been out of touch with our luminous liminal selves.

There *is* great news! As human observers at the focal point of an infinite possibility world, you and I are the ones who have the privilege to shape it by what we hold in mind. The boon of realizing the nature of consciousness as fundamental is that we can address problems at their source rather than through their effects – and thereby virtually eliminate them.

Leading humankind into a better world takes more than desire or even commitment. It requires knowledge beyond conceptual understanding, automatic conditioning, and fixed opinions. Let's take another leap here. It requires wisdom.

In the ancient philosophical Sanskrit text the *Mundaka Upanishad*, a favorite aphorism that I aspire to live from is "The sage must distinguish between knowledge and wisdom." Knowledge becomes wisdom when we are living it as the walking, talking embodiment of it. It is alive and pulsating.

There is a universal inner knowing in every one of us that there is indeed something greater, a higher intelligence that is felt as mystical and mysterious and irresistibly inviting. In this sense we have all at least glimpsed or flirted with liminal consciousness. Curiously, it has not been distinguished for us in a way that Edwin is making available so we not only recognize it, we experience it. And so liminal consciousness *as a distinction* until now has been largely outside of our awareness.

I call "The Art of Distinguishing – A New Worldview of Learning" a method of learning more suited to a quantum world. To *distinguish* is to bring something into our awareness in the present moment in a way that transforms our relationship to it. Distinguishing transforms knowledge from a concept or mental construct to a participatory experience.

Most people do experience a sense of their inner wisdom, spiritual connection, heartfelt compassion, and awe. We expect to feel those aspects of ourselves in religious services, during meditation, or enjoying the serene beauty and majesty of nature. These deeper experiences are rarely shared with others and have been virtually absent from corporate and business life. We keep them close to the vest.

Now we are in a time of making wisdom practical. A gift of this book is that Edwin Olson shows us how to make liminal consciousness practical, applying it to one of the most influential arenas of modern civilization – leadership, teams, and organizations. This is game changing.

In public conversation we are beginning to catch glimpses indicative of a sea change in awareness. It's showing up in leaders' relationships with their employees as the necessity to relate to the whole person and not just their workplace role in the company.

My partner, Alan Collins, and I have experienced this with our clients. Like Edwin we also recognized the exponential ability of business organizations to shape the direction and quality of life for individuals as well as for societal systems and structures. Thus, we focused our work with astute business leaders who had both the insight and foresight to sense that new thinking wasn't simply the proverbial "out-of-the-box" clever or innovative idea. It was a completely different perspective. When both/and thinking becomes a way of life we honor people, productivity, and profitability.

As you make your voyage through these pages you are sure to realize that the liminal state is a state of freedom, of creativity, of intuitive genius and insight where we connect to our highest nature. We also connect to our *non-local mind.*

One of the greatest discoveries of quantum science that Edwin addresses is the principle of *non-locality.* The universe and our minds are "non-local." A non-local universe means information transfers and connections take place outside the limits of physical space and chronological time. Our minds are also non-local, non-material, and therefore not "located" in the ordinary way that physical objects exist. Our mind does not end at the edge of our body and is not synonymous with the brain. This knowledge is invaluable for effectiveness. Since mind is not restricted by space, time, and matter, it can "go" anywhere to send and receive intelligence. The way I think of it – mind does not travel, it connects.

In liminal awareness, we connect to our non-local Infinite Universal Mind which is at once intelligent, accessible, and responsive. It is our own naturally occurring cosmic AI.

And so we return to where we started. What are the relevant questions arising in this liminal moment for humankind? How do we command with grace the revolution in technology? How do we create productive, profitable, and joyful experiences for the future of work? How do we cultivate awakened awareness in both seasoned as well as young leaders without a backward slide to either/or "thinking" that wants to abandon either the material or the spiritual nature of reality for the other? How do we develop a higher consciousness where "rules" regarding diversity and inclusivity will no longer be relevant because they won't be necessary?

Liminal Consciousness describes more than a philosophy or the latest business buzz word. It is much more profound. Edwin Olson brings this knowledge to us based on painstaking research of professional discoveries as well as his personal curiosity and yearning for truth. Whether or not we agree with every perspective expressed, the thread of its wisdom is impeccable. It describes an evolution in consciousness that can no longer remain hovering on the periphery of mainstream culture.

Kindness, appreciation, compassion, joy, love. These words, these virtues can no longer be excluded or put on the side of our culture or hoped for. They must be evoked. And they can be.

Liminal Consciousness is a priceless gift to every thinking human being, even to those of us who prefer to ignore the monumental season of change we find ourselves in. In unprecedented times there are at least three ways one can be with it: (1) hide, (2) adapt, or (3) lead.

The Hiders cover their ears and eyes and hope that everything will return to the way it used to be. The Adaptors wait for the circumstances to hit them unceremoniously and then try to make the best of it.

However, those who lead embrace with open arms the grandness of the date with destiny that lies before us. The Leaders become forces in the way we want evolution to go, to generate the way we would like the world to be.

We realize ourselves as practical instruments of creation, while at the same time knowing there is an Infinite Intelligent Field that calls to us with guidance. In the liminal state we can tune in to the energy-intelligent field that sustains us and take our wisdom to a higher octave. This book is a portal to take us there.

To borrow a phrase from the author who characterized his personal experience of liminal consciousness, this book becomes "an angel on your shoulder" guiding you through the promised land of your own intuitive, mystical, creative mind. You will enjoy it. You will expand from it. You will be delighted that you took the journey with him and with all of us.

– DIANNE COLLINS, creator of QuantumThink®

Consciousness Assessment

In his review of this book, Rabbi Rami Shapiro asks, "how can one mindset choose to surrender to another?" To discover if reading this book changes your current mindset, you may wish to complete this 10-item assessment. If you take it again after reading the book, you will be able to compare your scores. **Or** you may prefer to record your reaction to the five open-ended questions on page xxvii.

Instructions: *Choosing from a 10-point scale, record your level of disagreement or agreement for each statement. Then total your scores.*

Strongly Disagree	Disagree	Not Sure/ Don't Know	Agree	Strongly Agree
1 2	3 4	5 6	7 8	9 10

1. ____Mystical experiences are valuable sources of wisdom.
2. ____Business and government leaders need to develop their consciousness.
3. ____There are dimensions of reality beyond the material world.
4. ____Transcending differences is better than debate and compromise.
5. ____There is a non-material presence that I can access.
6. ____Moments of inspiration and dreams are from a consciousness outside of the self.
7. ____Human intuition can sense that something is going to happen.
8. ____Organizations must develop a higher consciousness if we are to survive as a species.

9. ____Transcending the material and empirical lets us experience what is significant in the current moment.
10. ____The new sciences and traditional religions both describe the same source of wisdom and love.

Total ____

Possible meanings of your 10-item score are on page xxxix.

Five Questions About Consciousness

Here are some of the things explored in this book. Note your responses to them as you begin and see how they may have shifted after reading the chapters.

1. What is your current view of consciousness?

2. Where do you think consciousness comes from?

3. What role, if any, do you believe consciousness plays in the quality of social interaction and discourse?

4. How do you see consciousness affecting what you deem significant in the current moment?

5. What similarities and differences do you see in how science and religion understand consciousness?

At the end of the Conclusion, you have the opportunity to revisit your responses to determine if reading the book had any impact on your views about consciousness.

Preface: Memo to Organization Leaders and Consultants

If you are frustrated or dispirited about the shallow level of change in the organization(s) you serve,
If you seek an innovative approach to change that will contribute to solving our existential crises,

If you want to learn new information more quickly, make better decisions under pressure, and be more creative,

Or, if you simply hope for greater self-awareness and consciousness about bringing about deeper levels of change for yourself or your organization, then this book is for you.

You can discover how using your "liminal consciousness" can reconcile your objective rational knowledge and your subjective intuitive experiences. *Liminality* is the in-between space and time that integrates our everyday sense of the world and the experiences that flood into our consciousness during meditation, dreaming, or other portals such as music, art, and nature.[1]

---

1 The liminal state is temporal, a middle state that creates a fluid, malleable situation that enables new creation. Victor Turner, "Betwixt and Between: The Liminal Period in Rites of Passage," in *The Forest of Symbols* (Ithaca, NY: Cornell University Press, 1967).

As you develop your liminal consciousness, you become more conscious of your unique mission and your imperative to act for the good of the whole. Being open to intuitive experiences reveals what is significant in the current moment and the possibilities that presents. As you become more confident about what is revealed through your experiences, you can forge new connections and networks that transcend the differences and the narrow missions of individuals, teams, and organizations. Life becomes easier, joyful, and more productive.

This book presents a theory of organization change based on what I have gleaned from my 43 years of experience as a professor, organization development (OD) consultant, and Jungian-oriented counselor, and my study of quantum sciences and complexity science.[2] I have also integrated my knowledge about the common ground of spirituality and science,[3] particularly the essential wholeness in the universe.[4] In my last book I argued that becoming conscious of wholeness was humanity's only future.[5] I believe this deeper, metaphysical approach to change is what is required to develop organizations that are able to meet the needs of their stakeholders but are also able to contribute to resolving the global social and political polarizations.

We all experience sudden feelings of awe, insights, or important dreams. Such events are indicators of liminal consciousness, the space in between waking consciousness and a "non-local" consciousness. Non-local consciousness is beyond the physical brain and body and not limited to specific points in time and space.[6] It

---

2 *Facilitating Organization Change: Lessons from Complexity Science* (2001), co-authored with Glenda H. Eoyang.
3 I am forever indebted to Rev. Charles (Chuck) Colberg, retired Lutheran minister, for introducing me to the religion–science dialogue.
4 *Keep the Bathwater: Emergence of the Sacred in Science and Religion* (2009); *Finding Reality: Four Ways of Knowing* (2016); *And God Created Wholeness* (2018).
5 *Become Conscious of Wholeness: Humanity's Only Future* (2021).
6 Pim van Lommel, "Introduction Nonlocal Consciousness." https://pimvanlommel.nl/en/pim-van-lommel/nonlocal-consciousness/

is a deeper wisdom in the universe that does not originate in the neurons in our brains and bodies. Tuning into and engaging with the deeper wisdom of Consciousness is needed to transform the complex systems we have developed.

Regardless of your current worldview about leadership, teams, and organizations, the principles and virtues that are developed in liminal consciousness that I present in this book can be a useful addition to your methods of change. The emphasis here is on – unity in diversity, equality, humanity, empathy, kindness, and love.[7]

As humans, we aspire to a still-wider conscious connection with a universal perspective, what Carl Jung called the "world soul."[8] For me, examples of these aspirations have become essential to my personal and professional journey. Please join me, dear reader, and entertain the value of liminal consciousness – while there is still time.

---

7 Nicolya Christi, *Love, God, and Everything: Awakening from the Long, Dark Night of the Collective Soul* (Bear and Company, 2021).
8 Ibid., 15.

Introduction: A Consciousness Worldview

Expanding the Current Worldview

The worldview of the nature of reality I am describing includes a "non-local" Consciousness that interacts with the consciousness of sentient life that is generally associated with the brain and neural networks. I encourage the reader to consider this possibility as a way of understanding soul, spirit, heart, and love – concepts that are beyond the materialist worldview.[1] Non-local Consciousness is experienced during meditation, mindfulness, and other methods that calm the brain.

I believe this worldview is a realistic and useful way to understand the energy fields and forces beyond the brain without introducing theism or other constructions of a higher power. I discuss this in *Part I – Developing Liminal Consciousness*. This worldview expands the materialist belief that consciousness is solely a by-product of the brain and neural networks. Some scientists, especially those who have had strong intuitive and mystical experiences, believe that consciousness is primary.[2] They incorporate their experience and the experience of others in their rational analyses: "deep inner

---

[1] Dianne Collins, *Do You QuantumThink?* (New York: Select Books, 2011), 59.
[2] Helané Wahbeh, *The Science of Channeling: Why You Should Trust Your Intuition and Embrace the Force That Connects Us All* (Institute of Noetic Sciences: Reveal Press, 2021), 80.

knowing meets evidence-based reason"[3] and describe the universe as alive, intimate, compassionate, wise, and spiritual.[4]

Adding a Liminal Lens

Liminality, derived from the Latin *limen*, roughly translates as "threshold." As used originally in anthropology, it means transitioning from one social state to another, such as the ritual initiation of an adolescent to adulthood. Think of all of the times you have transitioned in your personal and professional life. These events included liminal spaces – times of uncertainty, questioning, making sense of how to handle a transition and being on the threshold of something new but not quite there yet.

We are also in a liminal space and time when our intuition or emotions tell us that there is something more that needs our attention. We then make meaning by integrating these insights with our reason and logic. In this transitional state we gain clarity about how to interpret the present moment and what we need to do. For example, when I receive an insight which will change what I am writing in this book, I pause to have an inner dialogue about how to proceed. In these times I am in a liminal state between my empirical/rational and intuitive ways of knowing.

The Promise of Liminal Consciousness

There has been considerable research about liminal experience in organizations but not as a way of knowing.[5] Liminality describes

---

3 From David Lorimer, Scientific and Medical Network, founded in 1973. The network of scientists, philosophers, and theologians explore consciousness, spirituality, ecology, health, healing, ethics, love and wisdom, and dying in pursuit of a "transformative worldview for the 21st Century."
4 Gary Zukav, *Universal Human: Creating Authentic Power and the New Consciousness* (New York: Atria Books, 2021), 23.
5 Karl E. Weick, "Enactment and the boundaryless career: organizing as we work," in M.B. Arthur and D.M. Rousseau (eds), *The Boundaryless Career: A*

the uncertainties of temporary workers who switch companies based on projects, consultants who operate at the boundaries between multiple client companies, and entrepreneurs who start new ventures while still keeping their previous job. Liminality is also experienced by managers who handle interorganizational relationships within customer–supplier networks or company scientists who have strong ties with their scientific communities.[6]

These workers, consultants, entrepreneurs, managers, and scientists certainly have the kind of liminal moments I have described. My focus in the following chapters is to understand the vulnerability and openness of liminal moments that promote new perspectives, leading to a more nuanced and broader understanding of our common interest with others and how liminal experiences trigger reflexivity and learning[7] and the motivation to explore the broader and more inclusive world with a more open mind.

Qualities of Liminality

My NTL Institute colleague M. Francis Baldwin reports on her experience of "transcendent thinking" that expanded the scope of her career. She then lists the qualities that describe the qualities of transcendent thinking and, I believe, the qualities of liminal moments:[8]

- A presence that brings energy to those around;

- A "feel for" – a connection to people, organizations, and situations;

New Employment Principle for a New Organizational Era (New York: Oxford University Press, 1996), 40–57.
[6] Maria Rita Tagliaventi, *Liminality in Organization Studies* (New York: Routledge, 2017).
[7] Jonas Söderlund and Elisabeth Borg, "Liminality in Management and Organization Studies: Process, Position, and Place," *International Journal of Management Reviews*, British Academy of Management, 20:4 (2017), 1–23.
[8] M. Francis Baldwin, "Afterword," in Kate Cowie, *Finding Merlin* (London: Marshall Cavendish, 2012), 137.

- Generative thinking, transcending what is known;
- Letting go of mindsets that no longer serve their purpose;
- Translating the deep intelligence of the collective into learning and action;
- Creativity, play, dynamic imagination;
- Courage to move through fear;
- Investment in personal mastery as a life-long process.

I think of liminal consciousness as a self-creating field that is continually sending messages to my active mind, urging me to do good. (Another way of thinking an angel is on my shoulder.)

The more that individuals understand and collectively enter into the liminal inner stillness and experience of accessing non-local consciousness, the more they can liberate themselves from the demands of the individual and collective ego and become more conscious of community – to see that wholes are greater than their parts.

Liminal consciousness is developed in the mystical paths within yoga and Advanta Vedanta, Buddhism, Sufism, Christianity, Judaism, as well as humanistic psychology, transpersonal psychology, and integral theory. I believe that readers with knowledge of one or more of these paths will find that they are compatible with liminal consciousness as I describe it in this book. Each of these paths describe recognizing the non-dual experience of unity or one reality.[9] Liminal consciousness is a *worldview* that is an internally coherent way of making sense of life – in contrast to an *ideology* that wants to dominate other worldviews or ideologies.[10]

---

9 Connie Zweig, *The Inner Work of Age: Shifting from Role to Soul* (Rochester, VT: Park Street Press, 2021), 285–286
10 Ibid., xxvii.

The Need for Liminal Consciousness

In many nations around the world, their business, educational, religious, and government systems are not resolving social polarizations. The gap between super-wealth and poverty is getting wider. Global warming leading to greater climate changes is increasing at an alarming rate. Authoritarian extremists are trying to erode democracy. These crises have been amplified by the social media, cable news, and many politicians that promote an "us versus them" mantra. In quick succession, Brexit, COVID, the war in Ukraine, and the standoff on the U.S. debt limit have threatened the foundations of the global economy.

Rabbi Rami Shapiro attributes this dark night and global collapse that is confronting humanity to our "ethnocentric madness," our devolving as a species because we have not confronted our individual and collective shadows. Until we do, he believes there will not be a tipping point that will move us back to a "higher level of aliveness."[11] I believe Shapiro is asking us to develop our liminal consciousness, to engage the spiritual and moral shadows, and to transcend the divisions and fractures that have been created by mechanistic, materialist, and rational worldview.

In a time of rapid change and complex challenges, we need visionary leaders, cohesive teams, and transformative organizations. Liminal consciousness can unlock untapped potential to accomplish a collective purpose that transcends individual aspirations. If a critical mass of our business, government, political, and media leaders and change agents increase their liminal consciousness, it could reach the tipping point Shapiro hopes for. We may then be able to resolve substantial political, ethical, ideological, and environmental crises that threaten our survival.

---

[11] Rabbi Rami Shapiro, Beyond Big Religion: Perennial Wisdom and the Future of Spirituality, webinar by the Shift Network, *Mystic Summit*, August 18, 2022.

How to Use This Book

This book will likely expand your view of the reality of non-material, mental, mystical, and transcendent experiences. You will find concepts, practices, and examples that can be used to influence the direction of your groups and organizations. This enlarged view of reality is based on personal, subjective, direct encounters with a mindful universe. However, if you have not had such experiences, I only ask that you be open to learning the potential of liminal consciousness. If you develop confidence that there is a trustworthy, unseen, non-material reality and that you can receive guidance from such a source, you can be more certain about the choices you make.

The three sections of the book move from the theoretical to the practical and from the individual to the global. Based on feedback from reviewers, *Part I – Developing Liminal Consciousness* is important but difficult for readers unfamiliar with the research and dialogue about the nature of consciousness. If that is true for you, I encourage you to read a chapter of interest in Part II or Part III for examples of liminal consciousness and then return to Part I. The Glossary may also be helpful as you encounter unfamiliar terms.

Part I – Developing Liminal Consciousness offers an analysis of the experience of consciousness from scientific, philosophic, and metaphysical perspectives and how the liminal Self can be a positive force in the world.

Part II – Transforming Our Complex Systems describes the value of liminal consciousness for leaders, teams, and organizations as they develop creative solutions and cooperative relationships to serve the good of the whole.

Part III – Making the World a Better Place. The transformation envisioned in Parts I and II will require educators, trainers, consultants, and coaches who are committed to helping individuals and systems transcend dualities and differences and confront the social injustice and inequalities in societies around the planet. Enhancing current methods with liminal consciousness will develop organizations and networks that move societies to a greater global consciousness.

**Possible Meaning of Consciousness Assessment Scores
(The Consciousness Assessment is on page xxv)**

80–100   You agree that liminal consciousness is essential.

60–79   You are open to the contribution from liminal consciousness.

40–59   Aspects of liminal consciousness are of interest to you.

10–39   Liminal consciousness may be of little interest to you at this time.

Part I – Developing Liminal Consciousness

Our liminal consciousness accesses realities beyond our conditioned minds that often downplay the significance of experience. Liminal consciousness reveals expanded states of awareness without many of the restrictions of the human constructions of religion, society, and racial and gender identities.

Restricted views of reality were the inevitable result as the human species developed language, stories, and models of their perceived reality. This edited view of reality was necessary to navigate the perils of a dangerous environment, such as a possible attack by a saber-toothed tiger.

As I live and work, I count on my five senses and my analytical and logical abilities to be productive and happy. As I have learned more about liminal consciousness, I have become more aware of the inputs I receive from Consciousness and my engagement with a mindful responsive universe. I am more aware that reality is infinite, without form or boundary.

When I integrate my empirical reasoning and analysis of my brain with the insights I receive from Consciousness, my evidence-based reason is joined with deep inner knowing in my liminal consciousness. I am then more motivated to act for the good of the whole.

As Jungian analyst Murray Stein says, human development "moves like a spiral, coming back over the same ground again and again, but at increasingly higher levels of consciousness."[1] I believe this is a good characterization of the development of liminal consciousness.

Chapter 1 – The Reality of Consciousness. The human worldview is mostly an objective, material, physical world of people, things, pets, and weather. For some this is the only reality. When intuition transcends the five senses, there is awareness of a subjective reality – emotions, feelings, and something more. This chapter contrasts the two apparent realities and explains how the two are really one – a massively entangled manifestation of energy and information.

Chapter 2 – Experiencing Betwixt and Between. When we experience Consciousness, we move into a liminal state between our normal consciousness of a material world and a dimension of Consciousness. Experiences beyond the five senses and the conventional notions of time and space are known as "noetic" experiences. In this chapter I discuss how liminality naturally occurs and how we can intentionally develop a liminal Self.

Chapter 3 – Actions of the Liminal Self. A liminal Self is open to the process of change. When we learn how to reliably access Consciousness, we become open to new possibilities and opportunities. "Consciousness allows us to overcome the entropy that holds us in our comfort zones. Like a rock dropping in a pool of water, it sets up a wave pattern that laps against the walls of our stasis."[2]

---

1 Murray Stein, "Organizational Life as Spiritual Practice," in Murray Stein and John Hollwitz, *Psyche at Work: Workplace Applications of Jungian Psychology* (Wilmette, IL: Chiron Publications, 1992), 11.
2 From an early review of this book by Rev. Curt Ackley.

CHAPTER 1

The Reality of Consciousness

Physical reality is well known, although there is always more to learn. The physics, chemistry, and biology of the material world present a coherent worldview of reality. Less understood is consciousness, often called the "hard problem" for science.

The origin of consciousness is a continuing debate among scientists and philosophers. In this chapter I offer my understanding of the reality of a universal Consciousness, whatever its origin, and the connection to human liminal consciousness. Note that my references to human consciousness use the lower case "c." The capital "C" denotes a Consciousness that is universal.

Persons wedded to a scientific materialist worldview often denigrate any discussion of consciousness beyond that produced by the activity of the brain as "woo-woo." But "there are realms of existence and levels of consciousness that materialism is simply unqualified to pronounce upon."[1]

I agree with the worldview developed by scholars at the Institute of Noetic Sciences (IONS) and the Scientific and Medical Network (SMN) and others that universal Consciousness is beyond our five

---

[1] Edi Bilimoria, *Unfolding Consciousness: Exploring the Living Universe and Intelligent Powers in Nature and Humans*, vols I–IV (Shepheard-Walwyn, 2022). Bilimoria integrates the Perennial Philosophy with quantum sciences to broaden mainstream science beyond its existing metaphysical limitations.

senses, thought, time, and space. We become aware of Consciousness through our sixth sense – intuition. This worldview argues that Consciousness is "non-local,"[2] extending beyond the physical brain and body[3] and is fundamental, meaning that Consciousness is the non-material essence that precedes the physical substrates.[4]

Non-local Consciousness models allow for the possibility of the subjective experiences that are usually considered impossible by physicalist models or simply ignored because of the basic assumptions on which they are built. For example, in the scientific literature on near-death experiences (NDEs) people report merging with a larger form of consciousness that feels pure, infinite, benevolent, and fundamental, not at all governed by laws of neuroscience. Transcendent emotions like compassion, love, and bliss flow over them.[5]

The science of quantum biology provides a way of understanding how our brains and the nervous systems throughout our bodies interact with Consciousness. All of existence, including physical and mental life, is dependent on the capacity of electrons and protons in the atoms to be in many places at the same time. This is called *superposition*. Quantum computers, which are based on the principles of quantum mechanics, use superposition to process information in parallel.

Atoms and protons that have previously been together, once separated, are able to influence each other even when separated by great distances. This is called *entanglement*. These particles of

---

2 Helané Wahbeh, Dean Radin, Cedric Cannard, and Arnaud Delorme, "What if Consciousness Is Not an Emergent Property of the Brain? Observational and Empirical Challenges to Materialistic Models," *Frontiers in Psychology* (September 2022).

3 Larry Dossey, "Healing and the Mind: Is there a Dark Side?" *Journal of Scientific Exploration*, 8 (1994), 73–90.

4 Fredrico Faggin, "Consciousness Comes First," in E.F. Kelly and P. Marshall (eds), *Consciousness Unbound: Liberating Mind from the Tyranny of Materialism* (Lanham, MD: Rowman & Littlefield Publishers, 2021), 283–322.

5 Dacher Keltner, *Awe: The New Sciences of Everyday Wonder and How It Can Transform Your Life* (New York: Penguin Press, 2023), 235.

energy are also able to go through any material barriers. This is called *tunneling*.[6]

It may be that quantum non-local Consciousness is the omnipresent, invisible background that orchestrates these quantum phenomena from "behind the scenes." Coherence, as explained by quantum biologists, is that state of Consciousness in living cells where the quantum possibilities – electrons being everywhere at once – are essential for life. As the planet and the biosphere evolved, a dynamic state of harmonic resonance and spontaneous collaboration developed between the diverse elements and relationships of complex living systems.[7]

The ancient perennial spiritual wisdom has long declared that the world has one Consciousness of which we are a part. Founders of every major religion have experienced this oneness. Together, quantum biology and our spiritual/mystical/religious traditions present a compelling case for the reality of Consciousness.

Two is Really One

When we use language to make one object distinct from another, our brains let the object shine that we are highlighting. When we assign identity to a "cat," for example, we exclude it from all that is "not cat." Our experience introduces dualities which are non-dual. The presence of Consciousness is not obvious because when we experience dualities, the unity of Consciousness moves to the background.

Notice the two persons in Figure 1.1. Look again and you can see the figure of a vase between them. Think of the vase as the unity

---

6 Johnjoe McFadden and Jim Al-Khalili, *Life on the Edge: The Coming of Age of Quantum Biology* (New York: Crown Publishing, 2014). I use the quantum biology findings as a strong metaphor to understand body, mind, and soul in *And God Created Wholeness*, pp. 17–31.
7 Anneloes Smitsman and Jean Houston, *The Quest of Rose: The Cosmic Keys of Our Future Becoming*, Book 1 of the *Future Humans Trilogy* (Oxygen Publishing Inc., 2021), 227.

of Consciousness; the two persons are the duality. A mental shift is required to recognize something that is hidden.[8]

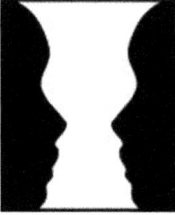

Figure 1.1 – The Hidden Dimensions of Consciousness

The quantum world is hidden from us the way the operation of the brain is hidden. When you think of the word "cat" and see it in your mind's eye, you are not aware of the millions of neurons firing in your brain in order to create the image.[9]

Einstein said that the emotional sensation of the mystical (Consciousness) and the awe and wonder it brings is the highest wisdom we can comprehend and is the source of "all true science and the center of true religiousness." The presence of Consciousness is an immediate and tangible experience. It is located in the stillness, silence, and timelessness that pervades everything in the present moment – beyond thought, beliefs, feelings, images, or imaginings.[10]

Everything is a part of the field of Consciousness. My brain and body, like a TV set, convert waves of Consciousness into ideas, images, and actions. Just as my perceptual ability of sight depends on my physical eyes, intuition depends on my networks of physical neurons. I see all of this as One. The illusion of duality comes in when I describe it. As the quantum

---

8 Ben Williams and Marjorie H. Wollacott, "Lessons from the Non-dual Philosophy of Saivism and Neuroscience: The Origin of Cognitive Filters and How to Reduce their Potency," *The Journal of Transpersonal Psychology*, 53:2 (2021), 119 ff.
9 Subhash Kak, Deepak Chopra, and Menas Kafatos, "Perceived Reality, Quantum Mechanics, and Consciousness," *Cosmology*, 18 (2014), 231–245. In Platonic philosophy the idea of "cat" would come from Consciousness.
10 Albert Einstein, "The Merging of the Spirit and Science," 108.

biologists have discovered, we connect to Consciousness through the simultaneous processes I listed above – superposition, entanglement, and tunneling. Consciousness "transmits wave information into the brain tissue, that ... is instrumental in high-speed information processing."[11] In my worldview, our liminal consciousness picks up information from Consciousness and communicates it to the brain.

Consciousness and Life

The Consciousness fields of energy and information connect to our human consciousness and all sentient beings.[12] People usually think that their ideas, insights, and images come solely from the brain. Alternatively, think of the brain and our five senses as a prism that the white light of Consciousness passes through and manifests as a rainbow of colors (Figure 1.2). The colors represent all dimensions of human consciousness. Reality is conventionally experienced in four dimensions: the width, depth, and length of objects and the fourth dimension of "spacetime." Consciousness is outside of all four dimensions.[13]

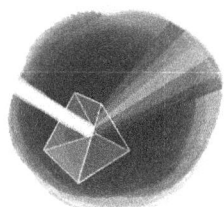

Figure 1. 2 – Prism Metaphor for Dispersion of Consciousness[14]

---

11 Dirk K.F. Meijer and H.J.H. Geesink, "Consciousness in the Universe is Scale Invariant and Implies an Event Horizon of the Human Brain," *NeuroQuantology*, 15:3 (September 2017), 41–79. Meijer is a professor at the University of Groningen.
12 Sy Montgomery's experience with an octopus was "an uplink to universal consciousness – an infinite, eternal ocean of intelligent energy." *Soul of an Octopus: A Surprising Exploration into the Wonder of Consciousness* (New York: Atria, 2015), 90.
13 Ervin Laszlo, *What is Reality? The New Map of Cosmos and Consciousness* (New York: Select Books, 2016).
14 Illustration by Tuesday Hadden.

John Hagelin theorizes that Consciousness is constituted of "micro-charged dark matter" which interacts with our bodies, surrounding us with an energy field that holds our thoughts and emotions. This allows us to think and respond without the constraints of our physical body. From this perspective, Consciousness manifests as a subtle quantum body around us that is made of dark matter, which is 90% of the universe.[15] This may be a way to explain auras, the radiation of a very low level of electricity that forms an energy field around the body.

Physicist Emmanuel Ransford claims that waves of electrons, when forced to become particles because they are observed or touched, "wake up" and make a choice about their direction, whether to swerve left or right.[16] This would suggest that there is intelligence and a psychic dimension in matter, even at the most fundamental level.

As an enormous collection of electrons, we also have choices to make and actions to take. As a metaphor, our inner intelligence, like the intelligence in the electron, is dormant and activated when we are touched by an outside force, be it a physical or a non-material force. This metaphor of the intelligence in an electron that becomes activated is an excellent metaphor for understanding that Consciousness functions like a fractal that is everywhere, infinite, without form, capable of infinite manifestations.

When we quiet our brain and reduce the distractions around us, for example, through meditation, Consciousness enlightens us with a greater measure of reality. I discuss this in detail in *Chapter 2 – Experiencing Betwixt and Between*.

---

15 John Hagelin, New Discoveries in Dark Matter and Subtle Energy Physics, webinar, June 12, 2022. Hagelin is a quantum physicist and president of Maharishi International University.

16 Emmanuel Ransford, "Can we Crack the Mind-Body Problem? Part I, The Galileo Commission," May 27, 2020. https://galileocommission.org/category/authors/emmanuel-ransford/

In 2001, I described the "massively entangled" parts of an organization as a complex adaptive system (CAS).[17] I did not realize then how deeply all of life and human-constructed systems are connected to everything – from the quantum level in the atoms to the galaxies. In a CAS, any person or part can initiate change by influencing the interaction of any of the parts. Since there is an infinite number of possible interactions, the resulting change cannot be predicted.[18] Even more so, the information fields of Consciousness contain endless possibilities that our liminal consciousness can access. We are massively entangled with dimensions beyond our comprehension.

As an analogy, the interacting parts and agents in a CAS that create new patterns, can be compared to the brain's dialogue with non-local Consciousness that forms the patterns in our liminal consciousness. Since Consciousness is a non-local phenomenon that manifests internally from the quantum field, a consciousness-based universe is entangled with living things. A dialogue may also be happening in other systems like plants and animals as they interact with non-local Consciousness.[19]

Clifford Warwick, a biologist and medical scientist, suggests Consciousness is like an old telephone exchange with its frantic switching activity. All of the true conscious input originates from those making the external telephone calls. If this analogy is correct, consciousness and self-awareness are not just the domain of a few – or one – privileged species. Warwick concludes, "if the living cell and not the brain is the conduit of consciousness, then arguably either

---

17 Edwin E. Olson and Glenda H. Eoyang, *Facilitating Organization Change: Lessons from Complexity Science* (San Francisco, CA: Jossey-Bass/Pfeiffer, 2001), 27–29.
18 Examples of change agent behaviors: counseling a leader, asking process questions, providing expert advice.
19 Charles R. Fox, "Psychophysics of Consciousness," personal communication, August 2, 2022. Fox argues that the dialogue in each system is mediated by a non-material transform function that results in a Useful Information Field (UIF) that constitutes consciousness at various levels of analysis. Fox is professor of psychology at Worcester State University and a fellow curator of the Galileo Commission Consciousness groups.

all organisms are conscious, or none are – and the answer cannot be none."[20]

Consciousness and Our Survival

If we view life through only our analytical, rational mind, our worldviews and interpretations of events inevitably become fossilized and non-adaptive. When we access Consciousness, we create conditions for something new to emerge. This expanded awareness of reality becomes our default position.

Aldous Huxley wrote that for our survival we need to access the mystical experiences of Consciousness, what he called the "Mind-at-Large":

> To make biological survival possible, Mind-at-Large must be funneled through the reducing valve of the brain and nervous system. What comes out at the other end is a measly trickle of the kind of consciousness that would help us stay alive on the surface of this planet.[21]

In this chapter I have argued that a non-local Consciousness is a presence that engages with our brain and body to form a liminal consciousness. The experience of this phenomenon is explained in *Chapter 2 – Experiencing Betwixt and Between*. Hopefully, developing greater liminal Consciousness will help us to "stay alive on the surface of this planet" as Huxley hoped.

---

20 Clifford Warwick, "Consciousness May be a No-brainer!" *Animal welfare-NeurologyOpinion* (January 10, 2023).
21 Aldous Huxley, *The Doors of Perception* (New York: Perennial Library, 1954/1991).

CHAPTER 2

Experiencing Betwixt and Between

Liminal experiences may be a transitional dream-like state as we awake from sleeping or a state to which we are moved with meditation, music, or other portals to a higher level of consciousness. In either case, they wake us up to a reality beyond ordinary real-time experiences. In this chapter I will discuss (1) how liminality occurs; (2) unintentional liminal experiences; (3) being intentional; (4) the importance of liminal experiences; and (5) becoming a liminal Self.

How Liminality Occurs

The Filter Theory. If Consciousness is fundamental and pervasive, connecting all sentient beings, why don't we continually experience it? Because our cognitive processes filter out a vast array of perceptual inputs.[1] We can imagine liminality as occupying a space between our human consciousness and Consciousness. To illustrate the concept, in Figure 2.1[2] all sentient consciousness, including us, is depicted as an entity with permeable boundaries that allows transactions with its environment. Liminal fields of consciousness form as life interacts with Consciousness. Liminal consciousness has

---

1 Ben Williams and Marjorie H. Woollacott, "Lessons from the Non-dual Philosophy of Saivism and Neuroscience: The Origin of Cognitive Filters and How to Reduce their Potency," *The Journal of Transpersonal Psychology*, 53:2 (2021), 119 ff.
2 Thanks to Amy Hadden for drawing this figure.

wavy broken lines to show its openness to Consciousness, which is the largest unbroken field in the universe.

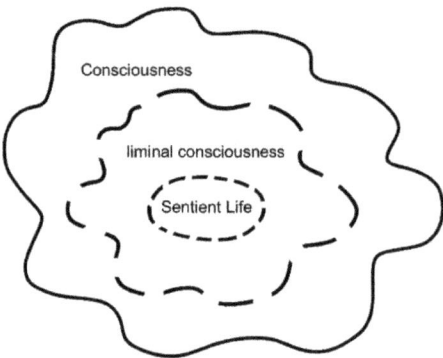

Figure 2.1 – Formation of Liminal Consciousness

When we turn off or quiet our conscious mind, we become aware of transcendent reality through dreams, visions, "eureka" insights, and memories. They don't come from molecules in the brain. They flood in from the field of Consciousness[3] and are accessed by the intuition of our liminal consciousness. The brain, which operates in the world of matter and spacetime, acts as a gatekeeper to slow down or filter the infinite amounts of information to which we have access. As a defense mechanism, it keeps us from being overwhelmed by what would feel like a fire-hydrant rush of water.

When we reduce the watchfulness of the brain, information from Consciousness flows in. For example, psychedelic drugs cause decreased activity and connectivity in the brain's connector hub, enabling a sense of unconstrained cognition.[4] When our active

---

[3] Neuroscientists continue to look for images and memories in the brain, claiming evidence of the brain's "wiring" being changed after a trauma. At the most, the change that is observed is the channel through which memories flood in from Consciousness (analogous to the "cloud" accessed by computers).

[4] From Helané Wahbeh, *The Science of Channeling: Why You Should Trust Your Intuition and Embrace the Force That Connects Us All* (Institute of Noetic Sciences: Reveal Press, 2021), 80.

mind is in control, we only take in what is salient and needed in the moment. To increase bandwidth, filters need to be removed.[5]

Vibrations of Consciousness. Intuition may connect to a universal vibrational field of energy when we engage in practices such as meditation to slow down our active mind. According to Raj Kumar, the reality that we experience is a manifestation of the rate of frequencies in which an object is vibrating. Every object, phenomena, thought, emotion, or mental state has its corresponding rate and mode of vibration.[6] Since the universe is also made up of vibrations, at the deepest level, manipulation of the vibration of thought can affect the universe.[7]

Spiritual and religious practices enable a connection with Consciousness through the vibrations of heart pulsations. By humbling the ego and connecting emotionally through the heart, intuitive insights arrive spontaneously.[8] I experienced this during a recent church service. At one point when the violinist was playing the prelude "Give Thanks," I felt pulsations in my heart. I was touched and opened to a flooding of Consciousness. As I reflected on my experience, I believe the vibrations from the violin raised the vibrations of my consciousness to synchronize with the vibrations of Consciousness.

Meditation, for example, decreases activity in the brain, enabling our intuition to receive novel insights. For me, this is similar to how unique patterns emerge from the self-organizing processes of a complex system. When conditions are "far from equilibrium" (to use a complexity theory term), they give way to unpredictable results

---

5 See marinacohen.com/silencing-your-left-brain.
6 Raj Kumar, "Vibration: The Cause of Our Existence and its Connection with Vedic Philosophy," blog, October 13, 2017. Kumar is assistant professor at the Dartmouth Institute of Advanced Sciences.
7 Ibid.
8 From Tina Lindhard, *Conscious Spirit Manifests Itself in Humans Through Tangible Heart Pulsations and Activates Primary and Secondary Perceptual Systems*, Academia Letters, Article 507 (2021). https://doi.org/10.20935/AL507. 4 ©2021, t.lindhard.iups.edu. Lindhard is a professor at the International University of Professional Studies.

— "the butterfly effect" (the idea that small, seemingly trivial events may ultimately result in something with much larger consequences).

Unintentional Liminal Experiences

After describing Edgar Mitchell's liminal experience in space, Larry Dossey, an authority on healing and human consciousness, pointed out that we don't have to be in outer space to experience these transcendent, transformative moments. These experiences intrude into our conscious life "in a dazzling variety of ways — in mundane situations such as sitting quietly, listening to music, viewing art, meditating, worshiping, praying, washing dishes, gardening, or doing nothing or they may occur in dramatic, desperate moments such as near-death or life-threatening situations."[9]

Throughout history people have experienced profound, beautiful, and transformative events as they connected deeply with the mystery, wonder, love, and energy of their liminal consciousness. When cosmologist and futurist Jude Currivan was four years old, she visioned being at the center of a vast interconnected and pulsing web of rainbow light. Since then, she has been conscious of "an infinite cosmic mind being dynamically co-created and experienced on multidimensional levels of existence."[10]

Liminal experience is really not mysterious or difficult. In both our waking lives and while sleeping it is "normal" to connect to another reality through our imagination, as did the author of the Harry Potter books.

> J.K. Rowling didn't agonize for years over the plot line for Harry Potter. In 1990, Harry, a black-haired, bespectacled boy, with green eyes and a lightning scar, simply floated into her consciousness during a delayed train

---

[9] Larry Dossey, *One Mind: How Our Individual Mind Is Part of a Greater Consciousness and Why It Matters* (New York: Hay House, Inc., 2013), 255.

[10] Jude Currivan, *The Cosmic Hologram: In-Formation at the Center of Creation* (Rochester, VT: Inner Traditions, 2017), 232.

ride from Manchester to London. She knew at once that the image of a strange boy in her head was a wizard who attended a magic school. It is as if Harry chose her, as the wands in the movies chose their wizards. She began writing furiously as the information flowed. In the years since she has edited and reworked those ideas into multiple books and movies, but the origin of the popular fiction series came from her liminal consciousness.[11]

Physicist Freeman Dyson also had a life-changing liminal experience while traveling. His "flash of illumination on the Greyhound bus" gave him clarity about the physics of elementary particles that had evaded senior scholars for years.[12]

Less-dramatic mystical experiences can occur when we enter a sacred place. I still remember the stirrings I felt when I accompanied my high-school friend James Motl as his parents dropped him off at a Dominican novitiate in Dubuque, Iowa to begin his life as a priest. The sounds of the singing in the chapel and the intense emotion of the moment likely were the beginning of my own spiritual awakening.

Persons with a religious worldview may call liminal experience a visit by the Holy Spirit, the voice that has flowed through religious scriptures. John Robinson, clinical psychologist and ordained interfaith minister, says that those who seek first-hand experience of the divine soon discover that the entire universe is conscious and alive, saturated by an all-encompassing and loving presence.[13]

Carl Jung explained how liminal experiences link an individual's inner psychic to an outer event. Both psyche and matter must exist in the same world, otherwise any reciprocal action would be impossible. Quantum

---

[11] Adapted from various 2022 postings on https://www.quora.com.
[12] Freeman Dyson, *Maker of Patterns: An Autobiography Through Letters* (Liveright, 2018).
[13] Adapted from John C. Robinson, "I Am God: Wisdom & Revelation from Mystical Consciousness," Progressive Christianity.org, October 22, 2022. Robinson is also an author of 11 books and numerous articles on the psychology of spirituality and mysticism.

physics could explain this as *entanglement* (action at a distance) where entities communicate instantaneously, faster than light speed. This instant linking of thought and a corresponding outside event is often surprising as it opens up new possibilities, a broader view of the world and the interconnectedness of the universe.[14]

Marjorie Hines Woollacott, a retired neuroscience professor at the University of Oregon, shared a synchronous liminal experience that occurred during the day she and her husband attended a neuroscience retreat:[15]

> I woke up as usual to shower, do hatha yoga, and meditate … [Later that morning,] as the talks began, I noticed that I could feel the same energy pulsing inside me as I often do in meditation. First, I began feeling it as a loving, softly euphoric energy in my heart – inviting me to turn inside. It then moved up to the space between my eyebrows, pulsating there as well. And then it shifted to the top of my head – vibrating, tingling – and there was a quiet euphoria when I felt it again in my heart. I was listening to the talks … able to understand, but all my attention wasn't engaged with the words. The energy kept coming into my awareness again and again all morning long … As we drove home, the energy was there – between the eyes, in the heart, at the crown of the head. It was so sweet, so satisfying, this … inward awareness as I watched the forest and the pastureland going by us on the drive.

Woollacott's experience illustrates how a liminal experience can occur at any time. Thomas Merton has provided a description of his liminal experience on the corner of Fourth and Walnut in Louisville, Kentucky:

---

14 Joseph Cambray, *Synchronicity: Nature and Psyche in an Interconnected Universe* (College Station, TX: Texas A&M University Press, 2009), 31.
15 Marjorie Hines Woollacott, *Infinite Awareness: The Awakening of a Scientific Mind* (New York: Rowman and Littlefield, 2015), 22–23.

> At the center of our being is a point of nothingness ... a point of pure truth ... It is like a pure diamond. It is in everybody, and if we could see it, we would see these billions of points of light coming together in the face and blaze of a sun that would make all the darkness and cruelty of life vanish completely.[16]

Merton dramatically describes an encounter with the light of Consciousness and the formation of a liminal space.

Being Intentional

We can intentionally use dreams, sounds, music, symbols, poetry, dance, worship, stories, and nature to have a liminal experience. All are potential portals to "a sense of awe, wonder, and beauty beyond a material, ego-driven worldview."[17] When we take in the beauty of nature, the chemistry in our body creates a new pattern. We let go of "must do" and open to the energy and oneness of creation.

As we become conscious of awe, our sense of self is transcended. In writing about nature, transcendentalists Wordsworth, Emerson, Thoreau, and others portray the self as dissolving during experiences of natural awe. Awe allows us to integrate into "larger patterns – of community, of nature, of ideas and cultural ... forms – that enable our very survival."[18]

Putting aside things that stimulate the brain, pausing, reflecting, paying attention to inner stirrings and quelling distracting thoughts

---

16 Thomas Merton, *Conjectures of a Guilty Bystander* (Doubleday & Company, 1965), 142.
17 Stephan Herrmann, *William James and C.G. Jung: Doorways to the Self* (Oberlin, OH: Analytical Psychology, 2020), 384. Herrmann is a Jungian analyst. I have discussed these portals in detail in *Become Conscious of Wholeness: Humanity's Only Future.* See "Part II – Accessing Universal Consciousness," pp. 33–74.
18 Dacher Keltner, *Awe: The New Sciences of Everyday Wonder and How It Can Transform Your Life* (New York: Penguin Press, 2023), 64–65.

will increase our creativity and insights from Consciousness.[19] Unplugging from smartphones, computers, email, TV, and any other devices that connect us to the internet and other distractions could be a first step.

We could also take more showers. Cognitive scientist Scott Barry Kaufman's research indicates that "72% of people get creative ideas in the shower. In a relaxing, solitary, and non-judgmental shower environment, the mind is allowed to wander freely, causing people to be more open to their inner stream of Consciousness and daydreams."[20]

The Importance of Liminal Experiences

Liminal experiences can transform an individual's life in substantial ways, often leading to a new career or change in their personal relationships, hopefully for the better. Carl Jung referred to such experiences as big dreams. Native peoples experience visions, often prophetic, that provide guidance for their tribe.

Accessing Consciousness as we navigate the challenges of daily life and work can help us see through the fears, resentments, pride, greed, and insecurities of the ego. When we are lonely, confused, or hurting, it is comforting to know that Consciousness is present and available to support, encourage, and help us to make wise choices. Abraham Lincoln called such aid the "better angels of our nature."

Some messages from Consciousness may be whimsical with no clear direction or meaning. For example, while listening to a meditation tape, I briefly drifted into sleep and had this dream:

---

[19] Lionel Corbett, *Psyche and the Sacred: Spirituality Beyond Religion* (New Orleans: Spring Journal, 2012), 222.

[20] The survey of 4,000 people aged 18 to 64 across eight different countries was commissioned in 2014. The survey also revealed that 14% of people take showers for the specific purpose of dreaming up a new idea, for fresh thinking, or for problem-solving.

> I am looking down into a large space, perhaps a cavern. I see three people standing in a row. They step into some special shoes and are whisked into a large tunnel.

When I awoke, my immediate thought was that the tunnel was a portal to the universe. The dream has lingered in my consciousness. It conveyed a wonderful feeling of transcending into a new dimension. As I write this, I am reminded of Dorothy in *The Wizard of Oz*, stepping into special red shoes, like the people in the dream, and being transported to a magical place.

As I reflect on why this is important, I think of the lesson Dorothy learned – the importance of community. The associations with dreams do not end. This is why liminal experiences are so necessary if we are to evolve our species beyond our current level of self and collective development.

We experience the totality of reality when we give up ego boundaries and experience oneness. If we see ourselves as discrete objects, separate and distinguishable from the rest of the universe, we cannot see the unity of the universe. In the past, sages and mystics experienced this higher state of consciousness and named it Enlightenment, Nirvana, or the Cloud of Unknowing.[21]

Einstein suggested that authentic mystical experiences may make the difference between a violent descent into political and environmental chaos and the transformation of the world.[22]

Becoming a Liminal Self

A liminal Self is always evolving in its transitions between the empirical material world and its connection to Consciousness, the mystical world of oneness. The liminal Self is a third world that

---

21 Kate Cowie, *Finding Merlin* (London: Marshall Cavendish, 2012), 37. Cowie is the founder of Wicked Company in Scotland.
22 Walt Martin and Magda Ott (eds), *The Cosmic View of Albert Einstein: Writings on Art, Science, and Peace* (Sterling Ethos, 2013).

brings these two worlds together but cannot be fully explained by either world. What connects the mystical and material worlds is intuitive and subjective. At the same moment, the liminal Self is aware of both the transcendent reality of oneness and the world of duality, of objects and fields in spacetime, a world of cause and effect.

As humans, we continually transition between the three worlds – material, Consciousness, and liminal.[23] As I observe our three cats, I believe they also transition between their three worlds – looking for action or food, cat naps, and dreaming with closed eyes and twitching tails.

What the ego finds attractive may not be what we actually need or an action we should take. Being receptive to the promptings of our liminal Self will open up more appropriate paths. We are invited to follow its lead, often with no clear idea of what it will be like. Lionel Corbett aptly describes this path:

> The particular path to which we are drawn is determined by a deep, intuitive resonance we feel ... with something inside us, a felt sense that is difficult to articulate. All we know is that we have an intimation of the presence of Something to which we feel called or drawn.[24]

Jeffrey Kripal, a philosopher and theologian at Rice University, describes the surrender of the ego as "the moment of realization beyond all linear thought, beyond all language, beyond all beliefs. *It is a very big deal*. It is often ... sudden, unbidden. It is also beautiful, elegantly simple."[25] Kripal calls that moment the *flip*.

---

23 The metaphors of "worlds" were inspired by Julian Caryon, *One Earth – Three Worlds* (Triarchy Press, 2022). Caryon postulates that a future science might be able to explain the intermediary realm [liminal] characterized by "the presence of oneness in twoness," with oneness [Consciousness] as causeless, the twoness [material] as causal, and the intermediate [liminal] as acausal.
24 Lionel Corbett, *Psyche and the Sacred: Spirituality Beyond Religion* (New Orleans: Spring Journal, 2012), 211–212.
25 Kripal, Jeffrey J., *The Flip: Epiphanies of Mind and the Future of Knowledge* (New York: Bellevue Literary Press, 2019), 12–13.

The "flip" is when the ego persona has accessed Consciousness and opens a path for the emergence of the liminal Self. I continue to experience the difficulty of the flip. Letting go of self-identities that have been responsible for social, professional, and financial success is not easy.

As Kripal says, being able to flip is indeed a very big deal. Yet it can be as simple as recognizing that our feelings, inner knowing, images, or symbols are indicators that Consciousness is surrounding us, and we only need to be open to it – something greater than ourselves.

CHAPTER 3

Actions of the Liminal Self

In Chapters 1 and 2 I explored how our liminal consciousness has developed as humans (and other sentient entities) experienced the pervasive Consciousness in the universe. In this chapter I explore (1) the imperatives of the liminal Self; (2) preparing for liminal action; (3) positive liminal actions; (4) liminal human interaction; and (5) showing up in organizations.

Liminal Imperatives for Action

Liminal consciousness often provides information that is relevant to what is needed in the moment. Whether we accept the guidance that is offered and modify our behavior is another matter. Letting go of unwanted attachments and gaining a measure of freedom from our persona can be difficult. If locked into a worldview and patterns of behavior that are not life-affirming; if fearful and resentful of our situation at home or at work, liminal consciousness can be a motivator to break dysfunctional patterns.

I believe that an impetus from the liminal Self is aligned with the energy unfolding on the planet that is driving an evolutionary rise in consciousness. Stuart Kaufman has described this impulse as the "adjacent possible," our need to reach out and move to new situations and territory to ensure our individual survival and the survival of our species. From my understanding of the Consciousness literature, I believe the adjacent possible also includes expanding in the non-physical reality of Consciousness. Growing our human consciousness is our imperative.

Preparing for Liminal Action

Developing this greater awareness is not easy. Although appealing in the abstract, my liminal consciousness can be threatening to my persona, my self-identity, that does not want to lose its attachments, beliefs, and status. When I engage with Consciousness, my liminal Self emerges that sees more deeply into the connectedness and wholeness of everything.

To prepare to receive and apply the guidance of the liminal Self, it is important to be curious about intuition and gut feelings.

- Inquire into the significance of the words, phrases, and symbols in a liminal experience.
- Adopt an attitude of learning, asking "What is this experience telling me?"
- Bring passion, integrity, fascination, imagination, and vulnerability to the process.
- Take time to let the novel information incubate.
- Value all dimensions of experience – sleeping, waking, when with company, and during self-talk.
- Find the miraculous in the ordinary.[1]

Anneloes Smitsman and Jean Houston describe how the universe is ready to help, but intention to receive and apply its guidance is needed. They point to our "latent capacities that many people never access or develop, because busy 'monkey minds' keep us preoccupied

---

[1] Thanks to Nina Fry-Kizler from the Institute for Noetic Sciences (IONS) for her webinar on heuristic inquiry.

with the surface stuff."² Accessing Consciousness while being simultaneously grounded in the awareness of our material self is achieved by working from a place of inner wholeness.³

Gary Zukav, the author of *The Seat of the Soul* and *The Dancing Wu Li Masters*, says we can intentionally ask for guidance from "non-physical teachers – impersonal energy dynamics that are always with us, know everything about us, and support us in our spiritual growth."⁴ This is how Zukav asks for guidance:

> Please show me what I need to know to live a life of joy and meaning no matter what I am experiencing. I am so exhausted from emotional pain and anxiety and stress and lack of trust. Please help me.⁵

Zukav points out that "a nonphysical teacher will not tell you what to do, but will offer you new insights, or show you possibilities that you might not have considered." We then have freedom to decide whether or not to accept or experiment with the insights.

Carl G. Jung reported his experience of gaining insight from "Philemon," a non-physical teacher, and other figures in his dreams and fantasies that "there are things in the psyche which I do not produce, but which produce themselves and have their own life:"⁶

> Philemon represented a force, which was not myself. In my fantasies I held conversations with him, and he said things which I had not consciously thought. For I observed clearly that it was he who spoke, not I. ... It was he who taught me psychic objectivity, the reality of

---

2 Anneloes Smitsman and Jean Houston, *The Quest of Rose: The Cosmic Keys of Our Future Becoming*, Book 1 of the *Future Humans Trilogy* (Oxygen Publishing Inc., 2021), 148–149.
3 Ibid., 156–157.
4 Gary Zukav, *Universal Human: Creating Authentic Power and the New Consciousness* (New York: Atria Books, 2021), 89.
5 Ibid., 39.
6 Carl G. Jung, *Memories, Dreams, Reflections* (New York: Vintage Books, 1965), 183.

the psyche. Through him the distinction was clarified between myself and the object of my thought. He confronted me in an objective manner, and I understood that there is something in me which can say things that I do not know and do not intend, things which may even be directed against me.[7]

Readers who understand and value Jung's contribution to psychology and human development will appreciate his reliance on a liminal experience to learn about "the reality of the psyche."

Positive Liminal Actions

The liminal Self has a great capacity for wholeness, caring, loyalty, selflessness, and for what is most important. The liminal Self doesn't ask "What's in it for me?" It knows what it needs to do for the greater good. When I am my liminal Self, I do not have to build, protect, or promote my idealized self-image.[8] I rely on insights that spontaneously occur and my dreams where non-physical teachers do appear. For example, while revising this book I had a dream that I could have easily written off as unusual, funny, and meaningless. The dream was:

> An ice cream shop offers an ice cream cone on Wednesday that has two scoops, covered with chocolate or other toppings. My granddaughter whose name is Tuesday requests a plain single dip cone. The shop owners call it a "Tuesday cone." It becomes popular and people request a "Tuesday cone." Some say, "I will have a double Tuesday," meaning two scoops. The owners decide to add a three-dip cone covered with toppings on Friday.

As I reflected on the dream, I came to believe "Tuesday" in the dream represented the value and popularity of living simpler and sanely,

---

7 Ibid.
8 Inspired by Richard Rohr, *The Immortal Diamond: The Search for Our True Self* (San Francisco, CA: Jossey-Bass, 2013), 7.

but society (represented by the ice cream shop owners) continued to create products with excess. I am trying to simplify my writing as well as continuing to lose weight. The dream gave me an image of simplifying my writing – less piling on sources that complicate the basic story I am trying to tell.

Liminal Selves experience and trust that there is a deep and consistent access to guidance from Consciousness. It is possible to switch from a problem-solving and analytic mode to a trusting, listening, and allowing mode. This deeper perspective doesn't require a focus on winning; we just need to be who we are.[9]

In her book on the inner work of aging, Connie Zweig says that to cultivate wisdom "we need the ongoing, direct experience of pure awareness, the unconstructed, empty fabric of consciousness, to progress on the path to direct insight of nondual reality."[10] This is the path of the liminal Self that leads to skillful and compassionate action. The liminal Self chooses "love instead of fear, each action of love instead of fear, each word of love instead of fear, each thought of love instead of fear. And more."[11]

Every culture has developed technologies, disciplines, and practices for liminal actions. The particular practice and path that individuals follow in those cultures is also influenced by gender, race, age, sexual orientation, religion, mental health, and social/economic class.

I encourage the reader to identify his/her/their best way to develop the liminal Self. It is urgent that more people evolve their liminal Self reaching far beyond personal dramas and self-concern to find creative solutions for the multitude of wicked problems we face.

---

9 Adapted from Richard Rohr, "We Are Being Guided," blog, August 21, 2022.
10 Connie Zweig, *The Inner Work of Age: Shifting from Role to Soul* (Rochester, VT: Park Street Press, 2021), 295.
11 Gary Zukav, *Universal Human: Creating Authentic Power and the New Consciousness* (New York: Atria Books, 2021), 99.

CHAPTER 3

Human Interaction

The four cells in Table 3.1 list some possible interactions between the rational and liminal Selves of two people.

Person A	Person B	
	Rational Self	**Liminal Self**
Rational Self	Be in conflict and blame	Avoid
	Experience I–It relationship	Discount out of envy
	Conduct transactions	Respect
	Exhibit rationality	Be cautious
Liminal Self	Provide help	Establish connection
	Be empathetic	Be compassionate
	Teach and learn	Create spiritual partnership
	Volunteer	Experience I–Thou relationship

Table 3.1 – Interactions of Two Persons

In the following discussion of the interactions, I will be Person A.

Rational self (A) *vs. Rational self* (B). There are many possible interactions when I (Person A) and Person B act out of our rational selves. The positive outcomes could include cooperation in accomplishing mutual goals in a series of transactions. Martin Buber describes this as a utilitarian "I–It" relationship. If both of us are in a negative ego space, there could be conflict, blaming, or just coping with the situation.

Rational self (A) *vs. Liminal Self* (B). If I (Person A) am in a negative rational state and interact with Person B who is clearly liminal, I may be envious of their serenity or discount and avoid the person, thinking they will only make me feel worse. If I am feeling good about myself, in a positive space, I would be respectful and listen but be wary about engaging with a person who is operating at a different level.

Liminal Self (A) *vs. Rational self* (B). If I (Person A) am acting as a liminal Self and dealing with Person B operating out of their rational self, I would try to be empathetic and helpful about their situation. I would be willing to teach and learn and establish a relationship and even volunteer to achieve mutual goals.

Liminal Self (A) *vs. Liminal Self* (B). If both of us (Persons A and B) are in a liminal space, it is likely we could form what Gary Zukav calls a "spiritual partnership, a partnership between equals for the purpose of spiritual growth."[12] Both would want to work and play together because of the elevated level of trust and the genuine concern each has for the other. Buber would call this an "I–Thou" relationship, a personal, direct, dialogical relationship where nothing is held back.

While I was making final edits to this book, Judith and I attended an art exhibition of our granddaughter Greta Olson.[13] We were struck by her mosaic titled "As Above, So Below" (Figure 3.1). As she explained its origin from her dreams, I immediately saw the connection to liminal consciousness holding the tension betwixt and between Consciousness (the hand pointing up) and human awareness (the hand pointing down).

The Hermetic maxim "As Above, So Below" traditionally refers to the correspondence between the spiritual and the material (heaven and earth).[14] As I understand the fields of Consciousness and our human awareness, I see liminal consciousness as the space in which they are integrated. When I interacted with Greta about the meaning of her mosaic, a liminal space was created between us to help understand our art and writing about the infinite in a new way. Our liminal selves interacted, equally and without boundaries.

12 Gary Zukav, *Universal Human: Creating Authentic Power and the New Consciousness* (New York: Atria Books, 2021), 100.
13 The exhibition was Greta's thesis for her B.F.A. from the Maryland Institute College of Art (MICA). See GretaOlson.com.
14 The Hermetic maxims are a collection of philosophical and religious aphorisms that are attributed to Hermes Trismegistus, a legendary figure who was said to be a teacher of wisdom and magic.

CHAPTER 3

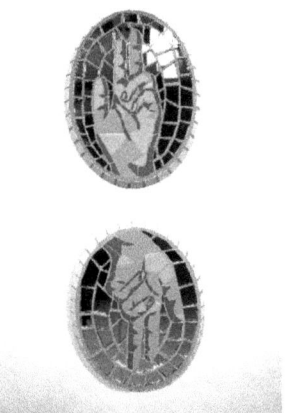

Figure 3 .1 – As Above, So Below

As we evolve our liminal Self, our thoughts, emotions, and inner wisdom also affect the consciousness of others. We become more inclusive of relationships "beyond color, continent, country, or kinship to conjure unseen futures"[15] that have the potential to expand without limit. When we bring truth, goodness, and beauty into the world, it becomes part of the collective energy of the planet, joining with the light brought by others to dispel the darkness.

Showing Up in Organizations

Self-awareness is an integral aspect of the field of organization development (OD). I learned early on in my training as an OD consultant that how I "showed up" in an organization and used my Self as an intervention into the system would be a key to success.

To effect deep organization change, the "self" that needs to show up is the liminal Self. The rational self would evaluate the situation through the veil of what has happened in the organization in the

---

15 Barbara Holmes and Donny Bryant, "Embrace Our Connections," in Season 2 of *The Cosmic We*.

past and not be as fully present in the moment.¹⁶ The liminal Self has insight on the future, the possibilities that could happen.

I often worked with managers who dealt with the financial and operational aspects but who also needed to innovate and plan for the future. I assessed their strengths and opportunities for improvement. Now I believe I would assess how often they only managed from their rational self. If substantial change is wanted, I would encourage use of experiential methods to develop the liminal Self.

Depending on whether a manager is operating out of their rational or liminal Self, there will be a different perception of and relation to reality with the potential to make either good or bad decisions. Together, the rational self and the liminal Self can help guide effective actions. Being in the liminal Self is a way of being, continually learning, defining, affirming, revising, and growing.¹⁷

Teilhard de Chardin's wartime letters to his cousin Marguerite Teilhard-Chambon are remarkable for a man working as a stretcher-bearer, living for the most part in the mud of the trenches, and at the same time taking advantage of his rest periods to jot down on paper his notes and plans.¹⁸ The following excerpt from *Writings in Time of War* captures the zeal and zest of someone who has developed liminal consciousness.

> Anyone who has the mystic's insight and who loves will feel within Something that seizes him and drives him on to absolute integrity and the use of all his powers. He is willing to self-correct and self-develop in order to become resonant to the pulsations of the rhythm of reality; the mystic makes himself docile to the unobtrusive demands

---

16 Ibid., 220.
17 Another model of "three selves" used by the Fellowship of Universal Guidance may be helpful for the reader. The three selves are: Basic Self (*rational self*); Conscious Self (*liminal Self*); and High Self (*Consciousness*). Wayne A. Guthrie and Bella Kavish, *Portals to Your Higher Consciousness: Exploring and Embracing Your True Selves* (Apple Valley, CA: Juniper Spring Press, 2017).
18 Pierre Teilhard de Chardin, *Writings in Time of War* (London: William Collins Sons & Co., 1968), 134.

of grace. To increase his creative energy, he tirelessly develops his thought, dilates his heart, and intensifies his activity. He labors unceasingly to purify his affections and to remove all blocks to the light.[19]

Teilhard de Chardin illustrates how liminal consciousness enlarges the heart. Focusing only on personal and professional success without a radical collective change at the heart level will not prevent an even more aggressive virus, environmental catastrophe, and/or social revolution from emerging. Our outer development must be matched with inner development. Kornfield notes:

> In Zen they say there are only two things. You sit. You tend the garden. You quiet your mind and open your heart. And then, with natural care, you get up and tend the garden of the world.[20]

When a critical mass of people have developed their liminal Self, there will be a shared experience of enlightened awareness beyond the personal ego.[21] We will recover a shared moral code "that cooperating, promoting the common good, is the right thing to do."[22]

To reach a critical point of global transformation, we will need a greater liminal consciousness in our leaders, teams, and organizations. I believe that teams, organizations, and institutions that adopt this wider view of consciousness will have a competitive advantage in attracting employees and customers who value their mission.

The next section, *Part II – Transforming Our Complex Systems*, may inspire you to help your group or organization be part of the movement.

---

19 Ibid.
20 Jack Kornfield, "Open Hearts, Open Minds," in Philip Clayton (ed.), *The New Possible: Visions of Our World Beyond Crisis* (Eugene, OR: Cascade, 2021), 208.
21 Inspired by Andrew Cohen, *Evolutionary Enlightenment: A New Path to Spiritual Awakening* (EnlightenNext, 2012).
22 Oliver Scott Curry et al., "Is It Good to Cooperate?" *Current Anthropology*, 2019.

Part II – Transforming Our Complex Systems

The complex systems and societies humans have created, including governmental, industrial, military, religious, and educational institutions, and all forms of collective agency are needed to reduce the threats to the biosphere, atmosphere, hydrosphere, pedosphere (the soil mantle of the Earth), and the noosphere – the sphere of consciousness, culture, and civilization.

This will require more than competency enhancement, incentivization, or goal setting from a materialist worldview. Breakthroughs in our existential crises of social justice will require a greater collective consciousness in the systems that control our destiny.[23]

In this section I discuss how liminal consciousness induces creativity and transcendence in leadership practices, team behaviors, and organizational missions. Opposing systems can be reconciled through mediating principles that synergistically and collaboratively foster emergence of creative events or structures that transcend the individual systems. Individuals and systems that act "on values that transcend the sheer material conditions and events of the world."[24] With transcendent practices comes an expansion of human

---

23 Ariana Rassooly and Param Srikantia, "Realigning Management with Social justice: A Case for Exploring the Hidden levers of Transformation." Unpublished paper from authors.
24 Peter B. Vaill, *Spirited Leading and Learning: Process Wisdom for a New Age* (San Francisco, CA: Jossey-Bass, 1998), 219.

consciousness that, in turn, changes our worldview, providing fresh perspectives, intuition, and intelligence to generate creativity.[25]

With greater liminal consciousness, leaders and teams in organizations and institutions have new ways of making sense, new ways of thinking and an openness to new ideas and experiments. Individual and collective egos can be transcended and contribute to the novel solutions that are emerging.

Chapter 4 – Leadership explores how leaders who develop a liminal consciousness are able to align their actions with a higher vision and lead their organizations to use their resources and power to foster the welfare of the biosphere and all of its inhabitants.

Chapter 5 – Teams explains how teams can develop a collective liminal consciousness that engages future possibilities and influence the larger organization. Team synergy makes the whole greater than the sum of the parts.

Chapter 6 – Organizations provides examples of how a manager's liminal consciousness can transform the consciousness of the whole organization and transcend the tension between material and spiritual pursuits.

---

25 Frederick Chavalit Tsao and Chris Laszlo, *Quantum Leadership: New Consciousness in Business* (Stanford, CA: Stanford Business Books, 2019), 174.

CHAPTER 4

Leadership

Management scholars typically regard intuition as the recognition of complex patterns that emerge from years of experience and accumulation of knowledge and the capacity to unconsciously process information.[1] Liminal consciousness is a deeper way of regarding intuition. It involves (1) integrating inner experience and outer behavior; (2) integrating the rational and the transrational; (3) developing creative choices that embody a social purpose; and (4) inspiring others to work cooperatively to accomplish a higher purpose.

Inner Experience and Outer Behavior

Liminal leaders explicitly pay attention to the dynamic connection of inner experience and outer behavior.[2] Leaders who bypass inner experience risk acting from an unacknowledged inner bias that distorts outward responses to situations. They may fail to see how judgments, assumptions, or biased emotions are distorting their assessment of the situation and ability to effectively respond. Or they may feel inauthentic, forced to act in ways that are deemed to

---

[1] Kurt Matzler, "Intuitive Decision Making," *MIT Sloan Management Review* (Fall 2007), 13–16.

[2] Lili Powell and Jeremy Hunter, "How to Recapture Leadership's Lost Moment," *Executive Forum* (Fall 2020), 51–57. Powell is at the University of Virginia and Hunter is at Claremont Graduate University.

be effective but that are inauthentic since they do not fit their inner experience or values.³

For example, political leaders who have previously shared their true feelings about an issue sometimes ignore their inner experience and feel compelled to espouse contrary beliefs to placate their constituents. In my doctoral research I found that members of the U.S. Congress, compared to other professional groups, had such a strong orientation to prestige, sense of achievement, and other indictors of outer success, that paying attention to inner experience could be difficult.⁴

Leaders who are able to move between awareness of their inner experience and outer behavior are better able to respond and adapt to the present moment. For example, in 2015 when the Supreme Court affirmed the constitutional right of same-sex couples to marry, leaders with a greater liminal consciousness, such as President Barack Obama, were able to say "a victory for America" and appear to be authentic. When John McCain voted "thumbs down" on repealing Obamacare, he likely was voting consistent with his inner conviction.

Leaders who only focus on tasks that are superficial and transitory find it difficult to be aware of the level of consciousness of another person.⁵ They may be successful in achieving specific goals but "the focused mind cannot extend down into the deep pool of unitary consciousness from which things are seen in a broader perspective. These association and broader perspectives emerge only when we take our minds off some particular tasks."⁶

---

3 Ibid.
4 Edwin E. Olson, *Federal Public Service Orientation of U.S. Congressmen*, PhD Dissertation in Government, American University, Washington, DC, 1967.
5 Peter B. Vaill, *Spirited Leading and Learning: Process Wisdom for a New Age* (San Francisco, CA: Jossey-Bass, 1998), 219.
6 Danah Zohar, *The Quantum Leader: A Revolution in Business Thinking and Practice* (Amherst, NY: Prometheus Books, 2016), 97.

Integrating the Rational and Transrational

Leaders who have developed their liminal capabilities are able to discern what is happening throughout the system and sense the underlying reality of oneness and wholeness. They integrate their knowledge of the rational material world and the transrational wisdom from Consciousness. They are a force for good, not only because they make a good economic business case, but mostly because of who they have become.[7]

In my dream the evening before writing this chapter, I was walking near the edge of a cliff while being careful to avoid falling over. I then encountered a deep hole in the mountain that allowed me to peer into its depths.

My interpretation of my dream is that it illustrated the behavior of leaders with liminal consciousness. In my mind, they are self-aware, curious, and spontaneous, yet careful to avoid falling into fanciful thinking that would be destructive. They take risks and find openings to provide insights for their fellow co-creators, not unlike a shaman in ancient times.

The shamans experienced a life force within themselves that energized and inspired them. They took inner journeys into Consciousness and brought back visions and the power needed by the community at that moment. Thomas Berry, the renowned spiritual ecologist, says the shamanic personality is emerging in our society and in the shamanic dimension of the psyche itself.[8]

Leaders who recognize their ability to integrate the rational and transrational are able to bring together disparate forces. Reducing the partisan mentality of our politics, ethics, and cultures could be an accomplishment of a liminal leader.[9]

---

7 Frederick Chavalit Tsao and Chris Laszlo, *Quantum Leadership: New Consciousness in Business* (Stanford, CA: Stanford Business Books, 2019).
8 Thomas Berry, *The Dream of the Earth* (Sierra Club Books, 1988).
9 Frederick Chavalit Tsao, "The Science of Life and Wellbeing: Integrating the New Science of Consciousness with the Ancient Science of Consciousness,"

CHAPTER 4

Developing Creative Choices and Social Purpose

By developing greater awareness of their life's purpose and how it relates to the well-being of those they lead, the environment, and the larger society, liminal insights can make a difference. Chris Laszlo, David Cooperrider, and Ron Fry, professors of leadership and OD at Case Western University, say this about the impact of research on Consciousness on our understanding of effective leadership:

> Consciousness research ... is shedding new light on the capacity for direct-intuitive practices, including meditation, art, music, and exercise, to transform a leader's consciousness as the highest point of leverage for entrepreneurial creativity that embeds social purpose.[10]

This research and my own experience substantiate what my mentors Peter B. Vaill and Lee G. Bolman have advocated: spiritual development and leading with soul gives leaders the passion and purpose to bring spirit to organizations.[11] Margaret Wheatley would add that internal guidance from a leader's spiritual self "motivates service, courage, and interconnections with all life."[12]

Laszlo, Cooperrider, and Fry conclude with this advice for leaders: "Take care of your inner self. Adopt practices that cultivate your whole person and increase your sense of connection to your life's purpose, others, nature, and the transcendent."[13]

Journal of Management, Spirituality & Religion, 18:6 (2021), 7–18.
10 Chris Laszlo, David Cooperrider, and Ron Fry, "Global Challenges as Opportunity to Transform Business for Good," *Sustainability*, 12:19 (2020), 8053. doi:10.3390/su12198053
11 Peter B. Vaill, *Spirited Leading and Learning: Process Wisdom for a New Age* (San Francisco, CA: Jossey-Bass, 1998), 188; Lee G. Bolman and Terrence E. Deal, *Leading with Soul: An Uncommon Journey of Spirit* (San Francisco, CA: Jossey-Bass, 1995). I fondly remember taking NTL Institute socio-technical systems and leadership workshops from Peter and Lee in 1974.
12 Margaret Wheatley, *Finding Our Way: Leadership for an Uncertain Time* (San Francisco, CA: Berrett-Koehler, 2007), 126.
13 Chris Laszlo, David Cooperrider, and Ron Fry, "Global Challenges as Opportunity to Transform Business for Good," *Sustainability*, 12:19 (2020), 8053. doi:10.3390/su12198053

Inspiring Others Toward a Higher Purpose

The concept of liminal leadership captures much of what recent scholars are naming as "contemplative" or "transcendent" leaders who have a spiritual connection. They inspire others to work cooperatively in the pursuit of a larger purpose that has been informed by Consciousness. In the words of others:

- Laurence Freeman and others say that meditation and contemplation by international business leaders contributes to their values of love, compassion, nonattachment, authenticity, self-knowledge, transformation, and others.[14]

- Anneloes Smitsman says that "transcendent" leaders enable collaboration, coordination, and co-creation for a thriving world and future, while addressing the greatest challenges of our time (*instead of exploiting them*). They are more aware of potential changes and the need to hold a space and support people during the transition period of uncertainty and breakdown.[15]

- Fred Kofman, the vice president of executive development at LinkedIn, also calls leaders "transcendent" who count on employees' need for self-actualization to "join a project that infuses their lives with meaning and significance."[16]

- Bengt Gustavsson argues that to avoid being passive, leaders need to transcend what is currently known and taken for granted as the only way to do business. When the grip of the current culture is released by transcending, the mind can gain a distance to the work and at the same time engage more in

---

14 Laurence Freeman (ed.), *Contemplative Leaders* (Meditatio, 2021).
15 Anneloes Smitsman, "Leadership for Tipping Point Times," (Sep 13, 2022). https://anneloessmitsman.medium.com/leadership-for-tipping-point-times-eb6da54533df
16 Fred Kofman, *The Meaning Revolution: The Power of Transcendent Leadership* (New York: Currency, 2018), 13. Kofman experienced a shift in his own consciousness that has empowered him to use resources and power to foster the welfare of the biosphere.

it.[17] "The individual evolution generates more holistic thinking, creativity, and harmony and culminates in a visionary state in the Enlightened Organization."[18]

Frederick Chavalit Tsao and Chris Laszlo also discuss the problem of the binding influence of what is known. When systems transform and give rise to new problems, a further shift in consciousness is required. What guides the process is the leaders' connection to the "deepest source of being, the force of creation."[19]

Reflections on Liminal Leadership

Liminal leaders can create the conditions that foster hope and faith in the organization's purpose. Rather than promote false certainty and telling others what to think, they develop relationships that create space for others to speak their fears and uncertainties and bring what they are passionate about to the surface.

Liminal leaders ask others to reflect on their goals, what they need, and where their insights are leading them. Motivated, respected, and loved employees provide socially responsible service to customers and other organization stakeholders.[20]

Leaders who embody a consciousness of wholeness and connectedness are likely more able to commit to working on global challenges such as climate change. Liminal leaders may embrace oneness in a pluralistic society in pursuit of business models designed to "do well

---

17 Bengt Gustavsson, *The Transcendent Organization: A Treatise on Consciousness in Organizations: Theoretical Discussion, Conceptual Development, and Empirical Studies*, Doctoral Thesis, Stockholm University, 1992, 323.
18 Ibid., 338.
19 Frederick Chavalit Tsao and Chris Laszlo, *Quantum Leadership: New Consciousness in Business* (Stanford, CA: Stanford Business Books, 2019), 49.
20 L.W. Fry, "The Spiritual Leadership Balanced Scorecard Business Model: The Case of the Cordon Bleu-Tomasso Corporation," *Journal of Management, Spirituality, and Religion*, 7:4 (December 2010), 283–314.

by doing good."[21] They can nurture revolutionary ideas that actually change and shift the way the world thinks and acts. They are able to interpret events and help clarify what is happening. They often reflect Consciousness outward to others as they become conscious of new options for action.

Most importantly, they do not act alone. In the next chapter, on teams, we will see that leaders with a liminal consciousness can develop teams that expand the vision of what is possible for the larger organization.

---

21 Ignacio Perez and Chris Laszlo, "Positive-Impact Companies: Designing Business Organizations as Positive Institutions," *AI Practitioner* (February 2022), 20.

CHAPTER 5

Teams

In this chapter I propose ways for teams in organizations to become kindred spirits in pursuit of the greater good for the organization and the world by raising their collective liminal consciousness.

Edith Sullwold has described a successful liminal process she experienced in a 35-member planning group that had to select a title for an upcoming conference. She noted that the "ingredients" for the success were trust in silence, in the "inner working of the spirit" in that silence, openness, non-judgment, focus of tension, and an intent to resolve.[1] I incorporate Sullwold's "ingredients" in three necessary conditions for a team to operate at a liminal level of consciousness: Intention, Hold Tension, and Patience.

Intention

A group that intentionally raises their liminal consciousness will increase their creativity and innovation.[2] Lynne McTaggart, an expert in the science of spirituality, discovered the power of conscious intention during her research with small groups that were sending their intentions for more peaceful conditions in Sri

---

[1] Edith Sullwold, "Mysteries of Change," *Spring*, 47:92 (1979).
[2] Wayne W. Dyer, *The Power of Intention: Learning to Co-create Your World Your Way* (New York: Hay House, 2005).

Lanka and Afghanistan.³ McTaggart developed a group process that begins with an intention statement. The group meditates and focuses on the intention for about eight minutes, alternating between silent repetition of the statement, which is sent not from the mind but from the heart, and holding an image of what is intended.

McTaggart believes the power of intention taps into the unified energy field of Consciousness with the intuitive group mind serving as the connecting link between the field and human consciousness. As the group seeks a deeper wisdom, creative insights beyond its agenda will emerge. I participated in a "power of eight" group in our local church that used McTaggart's process and personally witnessed the change reported by a member of the group. I became a believer.

Tyson Yunkaporta explains a process used by Indigenous peoples that could be a useful beginning for work teams that wish to use their collective power of intention:⁴

- The first step of Respect is aligned with values and protocols of introduction, setting rules and boundaries. This is the work of your spirit, your gut.

- The second step, Connect, is about establishing strong relationships and routines of exchange that are equal for all involved. Your way of being is your way of relating because all things only exist in relationship to other things. This is the work of your heart.

- The third step, Reflect, is about thinking as part of the group and collectively establishing a shared body of knowledge to inform what you will do. This is the work of the head.

- The last step, Direct, is about acting on the shared knowledge

---

3 Lynne McTaggart, *The Power of Eight: Harnessing the Miraculous Energies of a Small Group to Heal Others, Your Life, and the World* (New York: Atria Books, 2017).
4 Tyson Yunkaporta, *Sand Talk: How Indigenous Thinking Can Save the World* (New York: HarperOne, 2020), 247.

in ways that are negotiated by all. This is the work of the hands.

Respect, Connect, Reflect, Direct – in that order. Everything in creation is sentient and carries knowledge, therefore everything is deserving of our respect.

Teams do not typically develop a process to consciously access a deeper wisdom that is available beyond material concerns. It is easier to work with what they already know and what is readily available. My fellow OD consultant Sankar Ramamoorthy in India attributes this to the energy of desire, the pursuit of ideas and accomplishments that have a positive attraction and avoidance of those that are negative.[5] A conscious intention to learn how desire veils their awareness about what they are running after or running away from will keep the team focused on their true mission.[6] With intention to develop their liminal consciousness, a team can gain knowledge about their veiling of reality and avoidance of their larger mission.

Hold Tension

Team members often have strong opposing views when facing a difficult decision, developing a new product or service, or when going through a change process. If the team can hold the tension between the views, something new from the collective liminal consciousness will often emerge. These emergent ideas, although they may seem strange and unfamiliar, could challenge old assumptions to let the team consider new possibilities.

For example, a board of a non-profit organization was faced with a decision to keep or drop its board membership entrance

---

5 Sandarasubramanyan Ramamoorthy, *leela: A Play of Appearance and Presence*, 101. ISBN 979-888591297-6.
6 The ancient Indian traditions called this veiling of reality and projecting appearance *Maya* and the consequent polarization of attraction and avoidance create *Samsara*. Knowledge of this is considered *Moksha* or *Nirvana*, liberation from the world of appearances. Ibid., 102.

requirements. Some considered them discriminatory while others considered them essential for maintaining diversity and equity. Without much discussion and debate, the group held the opposing views until a resolution emerged to develop new inclusive criteria.

This is an example of Carl Jung's concept of the transcendent function,[7] our capacity to reconcile opposites by "transcending" to a higher level of consciousness through a synthesis provided by a metaphorical statement, new idea, or symbol that arises from liminal consciousness. When a viewpoint is challenged by an opposing insight, holding the opposing views as if they are both parts of a larger perspective invites new images that may point to a unifying position.[8]

Patience

A liminal team is receptive to gaining knowledge about what is possible. They create a space for individual and collective intuition to emerge. This requires patience, a willingness to wait to transcend their egos and move the conversations to a deeper level. When teams deeply listen to each other and intentionally not share what they know or think they know, they open a space of wanting to know, a sense of innocence about what will happen, a more vulnerable space for intuition to access Consciousness.

Andrew Cohen, a spiritual teacher,[9] conducts group sessions that encourage waiting to lower the individual and group ego and to activate the group's inner wisdom and their connection to

---

7 Edwin E. Olson, "Opening to the Change Process: The Transcendent Function at Work," in Murray Stein and John Hollwitz (eds), *Psyche at Work: Workplace Applications of Jungian Analytical Psychology* (Wilmette, IL: Chiron Publications, 1992), 156–173; Edwin E. Olson, "Transcendent Function in Organizational Change," *Journal of Applied Behavioral Science*, 26:1 (1990), 69–81.

8 See Barry Johnson's books for a comprehensive account of working with polarities: *And: Making a Difference by Leveraging Polarity, Paradox or Dilemma*, vols 1 and 2 (2020, 2021).

9 Author of *Evolutionary Enlightenment: A New Path to Spiritual Awakening* (EnlightenNext, 2012). https://www.manifest-nirvana.com

Consciousness.[10] I experienced one of Cohen's Zoom group sessions. The rules the group followed to achieve a place of coherence and deep wisdom reminded me of the practice of passing around a "talking stick," an instrument of Aboriginal democracy used by many tribes. The rules for patient dialogue that I experienced were:

1. *Keep ego out of the picture.* Be more interested in what I don't know than what I do know. Say to yourself, "I don't already know but I want to learn."

2. *Pay attention and listen with intensity, don't judge.* (A team member could ask, "How am I contributing to the disorder in the team?" to become more responsible and liberated from ego.)

3. *Say something if you are moved to.* Listen with intensity to what is needed, not what I want and only speak if you have to. (Do not edit, judge, or argue with any promptings you receive. Discerning the meaning and value of the message may take time.)

4. During the session, *everyone speaks out at least once* when they feel they are fully present.

After only a few minutes, I experienced a relaxed and open atmosphere in the Zoom group. I felt a numinous presence, a sense of love, peace, and connection. The comments from group members seemed to come from a deep place.

Then one member talked from what was clearly an ego place. I felt that a group spirit had left the group. I mentally checked out for about 20 minutes. I struggled to get back to a liminal state. When I did recover a sense of the liminal, I reflected that a liminal group can continuously reinvent itself through moment-to-moment mutual understanding.[11]

---

10 From a Zoom course by Andrew Cohen, 2022.
11 James E. Beichler, "Aspects of Consciousness: Theoretical, Spiritual, Anomalous, Experiential" (2018 ASCSI Annual Conference, Raleigh, NC).

Obstacles to Liminality

When team leaders and members are initially advised that their team needs to slow down, pause, and take time to be quiet and reflect, they are likely to be skeptical. Not talking, in their minds, would mean that the team isn't working. True, during quiet times the brain does slow down, but in return, images and creative solutions from Consciousness become available.

Other obstacles to working in a liminal space include: unwillingness to face conflict that may arise; reluctance to sustain the tension until a more comprehensive vision appears; failure to give the message from liminal consciousness enough value and time; lack of courage to take risks; and/or an unwillingness to obtain help and guidance in integrating the new wisdom.

To help overcome these obstacles, group facilitators or leaders could ask questions such as: What were the things like in the origin of this group? What are the things we believe about ourselves? What gifts do you bring to the group? What would be deemed blasphemies in the organization? What will we be in two years from now? Such questions probe the assumptions and polarities within the group and stir and harness the energy of the transcendent function to transform organizational struggles into new ways of perceiving and thinking.

The Value of Liminal Groups

My experience with liminal groups has convinced me that such groups can be catalysts for change in the larger organization, leading to unexpected outcomes. I have experienced this in the T-groups of the NTL Institute and several adult study groups in churches. Rather than talk to show how smart they were, the members patiently waited and only spoke when they sensed that they had something important to contribute, most likely something streaming from Consciousness.

Teams will have big ideas, breakthroughs, and new visions if they are open to their present awareness to *"receive* the larger truths of life" rather than believing they can *wrest* these larger truths through intense, sustained effort.[12]

Big ideas and breakthroughs can only come to us in the present. Managerial teams that are locked into their plans or exhausted by the anxieties of a current crisis and without energy for its situation will not receive a new vision for the organization.[13] They also will not be able to create a space of co-creating to connect across projects with other teams in and outside of the organization.

Comparison to High-Performing Teams

I began this chapter by identifying three necessary conditions for a successful liminal team: the team needs to (1) intentionally access Consciousness; (2) hold any tensions that arise; and (3) patiently wait for the emergence of a unifying position. But how do they compare to other high-performing teams?

Liminal teams share many of the attributes and behaviors of other effective teams. However, there is a significant difference. Table 5.1 compares the attributes of the "Dream Teams" identified by journalist Shane Snow with what we may expect to find in a liminal team.[14]

---

12 Peter B. Vaill, *Spirited Leading and Learning: Process Wisdom for a New Age* (San Francisco, CA: Jossey-Bass, 1998), 237.
13 Ibid.
14 Shane Snow, *Dream Teams: Working Together Without Falling Apart* (New York: Portfolio, 2018). The attributes of the Dream Teams are "eight counterintuitive lessons" Snow learned while writing the book.

Dream Team	Liminal Team
Has a shared vision but is flexible in its strategy	Vision and strategy are grounded in the team's intuition of reality and the greater good
Team leader has strong opinions but is adaptable	Leadership is shared and responds to the reality of the moment
Different ideas and diverse ways of thinking are integrated	Ideas and images emerge through the transcendent function (Jung)
Knows when and when not to change its viewpoint	Change of viewpoint emerges from the interactions
Team has shared goals but not necessarily shared values	Team goals and values are responsive to the needs of the greater whole
Has conflict of ideas but provides full personal and emotional support	Differences are resolved as resolutions evolve from Consciousness
"Good trouble" and opposition are supported	Contrasting views are integrated through the transcendent function
Optimism is combined with skepticism	Team integrates the differences of the parts in the whole

Table 5.1 – Comparison of a "Dream Team" and a Liminal Team

So, what is the significant difference? Both teams in Table 5.1 appear to be agile, engaged, and resilient, able to sense and respond to what is important, and be aware of their biases. As I review and reflect on the contrasting attributes, I sense that the hearts and minds of a liminal team are synchronized and aligned. There appears to be an organic flow as they transcend individual agendas and egos, engage in open dialogue, and leverage their diverse skill sets to address complex challenges.

Carl Jung said that responding to liminal material is like a dialogue between two persons "with equal rights, each of whom gives the other credit for a valid argument and considers it worthwhile to modify the conflicting standpoints."[15] The dialogue in a liminal

---

15 Carl G. Jung, "The Transcendent Function," in *Collected Works*, 8: 67–91 (New York: Pantheon, 1916), par. 186.

team is more likely about what outcome will aid the flourishing of the greater whole which could be the parent organization, the society, and/or the Earth.

The examples in *Chapter 6 – Organizations* expand the scope of understanding how liminality can make a significant difference in the workplace.

CHAPTER 6

Organizations

Liminality in organizations can take many forms. In this chapter I will explore its expression as (1) Spirit; (2) Transcendence; (3) Total Interconnectedness; (4) Higher Purpose; and (5) Practical Way of Working.

Spirit

In 2010 I authored an article about "spirit" in organizations, "The Vital Dimension of Social Change."[1] In the article I argued that the spirit in organization is manifested with actions and care that strengthen connections, enrich relationships, and actualize a higher purpose that serves the greater good.

Now after 12 years of researching and publishing books on the nature of reality, our ways of knowing, wholeness, and consciousness,[2] I have a broader understanding of "spirit" and how it is vital in organizational and social change. The need for more spiritually inclined workplaces is greater than ever. According to a Flex Jobs survey of 2,000 people in early 2022, the number one reason Americans are

---

[1] Edwin E. Olson, "The Vital Dimension of Social Change," *Practising Social Change* (Washington, DC: NTL Institute, 1:1, 2010).
[2] See *Finding Reality, And God Created Wholeness*, and *Become Conscious of Wholeness* in the biography.

quitting their jobs is "toxic company culture" (62%), followed by low salary (59%), and a lack of healthy work–life balance (49%).[3]

Organizations that develop a deeper sense of meaning and greater appreciation and respect among their members would reduce toxicity in the workplace, foster more equitable salaries, and reset the work–life balance. Workplace spirituality helps members to transcend their egos[4] and connect with others around values and issues that are important to them, thus creating a sense of inclusion and belonging.[5]

Transcendence

Just as individuals transcend their egos and limiting beliefs as they evolve, organizations can transcend their self-imposed limits and patterns. Both individuals and organizations can creatively develop new levels of complexity and thus new degrees of relatedness.[6]

To my knowledge, the first academic discussion of a transcendent secular organization was in a 1992 business dissertation. Bengt Gustavsson, then a student and thereafter a professor at the Stockholm University, argued that organizations need to transcend to more abstract and holistic levels that unite mind and matter, as suggested by quantum physics.[7]

Gustavsson concluded that the level of the collective consciousness of the organization is evident in the goals, vision, and culture of

---

3 Rachel Pelta, "Great Resignation: Survey Finds 1 in 3 are Considering Quitting Their Jobs," reported in *Axios*, 2022.
4 D.W. McCormack, "Spirituality and Management," *Journal of Managerial Psychology*, 9:6 (1994), 461–476.
5 Mary Ann Hazen and Jo Anne Isbey, "Images of the Intrapersonal Organization: Soul Making at Work," *Interpersonal Journal of Transpersonal Studies*, 23:1 (2004).
6 Ilia Delio, *The Hours of the Universe: Reflections on God, Science, and the Human Journey* (Maryknoll, NY: Orbis Books, 2021), 201.
7 Bengt Gustavsson, *The Transcendent Organization: A Treatise on Consciousness in Organizations: Theoretical Discussion, Conceptual Development, and Empirical Studies*, Doctoral Thesis, Stockholm University, 1992.

the organization. At higher levels of consciousness, the ego of the organization and the drive for material success diminish and a spiritual motive arises.[8] Members do what they love, and they feel they are making a contribution.

In a later article, Gustavsson advocated for a new paradigm based on a new science of consciousness in order to do justice to the vast potential of human consciousness.[9] Such a paradigm will include liminality as a way to guide the integration of the organization's need for material and competitive success with a commitment to contribute to the greater society.

The concept of a transcendent organization includes the possibility that an organization Mind is unconsciously generated that results in old and outdated habits and patterns of thinking and conclusions.[10]

In evaluating the hypothesis that there is an organization Mind or consciousness, Australian OD consultant Helen Russ and her colleagues led several group sessions in three organizations. They facilitated a liminal state of stillness (being receptive and internally quiet) in the groups that was a portal to "noetic" consciousness (inner wisdom, direct knowing, intuition, implicit understanding).[11]

Russ compared the mission statements developed by these groups with the mission statements posted on the organization websites. The corporate mission statement on the website of an emergency service organization was "to enhance community safety, quality of life, and confidence by minimizing the impact of hazards and emergency incidents on the people, environment, and economy." The mission statement written by a group that received the noetic

---

8 Ibid.
9 Bengt Gustavsson, "Towards a Transcendent Epistemology of Organizations: New Foundations for Organizational Change," *Journal of Organizational Change Management* (August 2001). ISSN: 0953-4814.
10 Dianne Collins, "You Can't Get 'There' from 'Here:' Why Change Doesn't Work," blog. QuantumThink.com
11 Helen Russ, "Metaphysical Mapping: A Methodology to Map the Consciousness of Organizations," *Methodological Innovations*, Sage (May–August 2018), 1–14. Definition of "noetic" is from the Institute of Noetic Sciences (IONS),

training included "there is strength, efficiency, and the future in collaboratively protecting what is created together."[12]

Notice that the corporate mission emphasized the outcomes of reducing hazards. The group's mission characterized the collaborative process. Which is more inspiring?

Russ believes that the noetic groups contacted the organizational consciousness or archetype, which she calls its "Lex," its living Form.[13] When organizations operate at noetic levels of consciousness, they can retain the connection between the mission statement and its living Form.

Russ's work suggests that when a transcendent organization's members are connected with the organization archetype (consciousness), the life and dynamism of the archetype is reflected in systems, operations, and programs. She declares that until members of an organization recognize the spirit of the organization as a life Form in its own rights, change programs will only make marginal change.

Total Interconnectedness

Some organizations are striving to be more "conscious." Futurist and business visionary John Renesch describes such an organization as pursuing greater depths of change by becoming a learning organization committed to "becoming [as] self-aware and responsible as it can at any given time in its life."[14] It focuses on "cleaning up an unwanted quality, procedure, practice, or other element of its culture."

Some organizations have adopted methods that will engage greater liminality. For example, Google has a popular course on mindfulness

---

12 Ibid., 10.
13 Helen Russ, "Lexion: That Which Upholds or Bears an Archetype: Introducing Lex and Lexion to Modern English," *Advances in Language and Literary Studies*, 6:6 (December 2015), 94–100.
14 John Renesch, "The Conscious Organization: Workplace for the Self-Actualized," *Spanda Journal* (2012), 227. In a reprinted slightly revised version in 2020 the subtitle was changed to "Workplace for the *Self-Transcended*." Italics added.

and compassion, "Search Inside Yourself," that is offered four times a year. It teaches Google's employees how to apply mindfulness techniques in the workplace.[15]

Rich Fernandez, the senior people development lead at Google, says that reflective practices are critical to organizational success. "To be a truly enduring company, to succeed in complex and rapidly changing environments, people need to take on many perspectives. You have to have multiple world-changing insights and innovations on a sustained basis. So, you need to have a set of practices that renews and bolsters you throughout that journey."[16]

The most extensive example of a transcendent organization is provided by Anil K. Maheshwari. He discusses an organization that transcends surface reality and taps the potential for growth and abundance from a higher consciousness. In his model of "Higher Consciousness Management" (HCM) the leader provides a high-aspirational moral vision through values, principles, purposes, and modeling a higher moral consciousness.[17]

Maheshwari provides a case of an IT back-office organization based in India that grew rapidly to 10 times its expected size, or 3,000 employees, in a notably non-business-friendly state of India. The CEO led the organization in the spirit of *Vasudhaiva Kutumbakam*, that the entire world is one family – a philosophy of total interconnectedness. The outcome of implementing this philosophy is described by Maheshwari:

> Talented employees gravitated to this company because of its nurturing practices and rapid growth. The CEO saw the Vedic wisdom of expanding the circle of care by engaging not only the employees but also their families.

---

15 Ignacio Perez and Chris Laszlo, "Positive-Impact Companies: Designing Business Organizations as Positive Institutions," *AI Practitioner* (February 2022), 21.
16 Ibid.
17 Anil K. Maheshwari, "Higher Consciousness Management: Transcendence for Spontaneous Right Action," *Journal of Management, Spirituality & Religion*, 18:6 (2021), 77–91.

CHAPTER 6

> All managers were given a parental role of maintaining a personal touch with their direct reports and their families. This relationship deepened the bonds between the employees and the company such that the employees' families would not approve of their leaving the company. ... The CEO deftly engaged the trade unions from his Vedic approach, and eventually persuaded them that this was an essential service for customers around the world. This CEO openly shared the company's playbook with competitors and partnered with its competition and other giants of the industry in its community to grow the overall business in the region. Even the auditors of the company were treated as friends, with the expectation that the audit process will lead to identifying greater opportunities for improvement of the organization. Gradually, the employees began to believe that this company was their dream career destination and there was a very low attrition rate. The employees gave their full dedication to the company and recommended others to join the company.

Maheshwari urges leaders to expand their own consciousness through transcendence interaction workshops, including concepts such as "consciousness, soul work, and organizational spirituality."[18] He acknowledges the importance of the credibility of the top leader and that leaders who view organizations through a material lens will require an evidence-based business case in order to invest in this process.

I agree that adopting a philosophy such as total interconnectedness would be heavily dependent on the worldview and credibility of the top leader. Such an approach also needs to be acceptable in the culture of the society. In the case presented by Maheshwari, the Vedic consciousness of the CEO has wide support in India. Optimistically, since every culture, including totalitarian countries,

18 Ibid.

have one or more spiritual dimensions, working with one of those traditions could help organizations in that society to be more liminal.

Higher Purpose

In his early writing, Abraham Maslow argued that after we have satisfied our basic needs for survival and security, our highest desire is to self-actualize, to become the most that we can be. But in his later years Maslow went beyond the boundary of self-actualization to transcendence. He defined transcendence as

> the very highest and most inclusive or holistic levels of human consciousness, behaving and relating, as ends rather than means, to oneself, to significant others, to human beings in general, to other species, to nature, and to the cosmos.[19]

Maslow came to realize that transcendence was a natural extension of self-actualization. He recognized transcendent behaviors in moving beyond weaknesses, fears, and dependency; transcending the opinions or expectations of others; and achieving a sense of unity with oneself, others, and a higher power.[20]

If transcendence is a natural extension of self-actualization for individuals, can the same be said for organizations? Václav Havel, the former president of the Czech Republic, offers this goal which is within reach of our organizations: "We should seek new ways to *restore the feeling for what transcends humanity*, for what gives meaning to the world surrounding it, as well as to human life itself."[21]

---

19 Abraham H. Maslow, "Various Meanings of Transcendence," in The Farther Reaches of Human Nature (New York: Penguin, 1993).
20 Abraham H. Maslow, *Maslow on Management* (New York: Wiley, 1998).
21 Excerpt from Václav Havel, "A Sense of the Transcendent." This essay was first given as a talk to the National Press Club, Canberra, Australia, March 29, 1995 and is included in a collection of his essays, *The Art of the Impossible: Politics as Morality in Practice* (New York: Knopf, 1997). Italics added to emphasize the transcendent.

CHAPTER 6

What transcends humanity is Love, the invisible strong force of attraction which Brian Swimme calls "the urge to merge."[22] Marcel Schwantes, an executive coach, describes how Love animates the workplace:

> The word "love," in a leadership-at-work sense, is not a feeling – it's a verb; it's packed with action. It shows up in meeting the needs of others to get results, clearing obstacles from people's path, and empowering others to succeed as workers and human beings. It has intrinsic value for both leader and employee.[23]

Transcendent organizations are in service of a higher purpose. In the context of our national and global crises and conflicts, they have the greatest potential for resolving our polarities and developing a higher global consciousness that will move societies beyond the bounds of culture, religion, nation, ethnic group, and gender.

How leaders currently make meaning and examine existing assumptions in organizations is mostly within the materialist paradigm. Most of what happens is transactional. Agreements are made to work together to accomplish a set of objectives and larger goals.

Sean Kelly, a professor of philosophy, cosmology, and consciousness, states that we are in a process of transformation that is inherently spiritual or transcendent in nature. "Avoiding denying, or otherwise diluting the full force of the process risks aborting the new identity struggling to be born."[24] A renewed dedication to transcendence has

---

22 Brian Swimme, *The Universe Story: From the Primordial Flaring Forth to the Ecozoic Era – A Celebration of the Unfolding of the Cosmos* (New York: HarperOne, 1994). My son, Eric A. Olson, associate professor of science education at SUNY-Oswego, upon reading this discussion of Love proclaimed, "Love is also LOTS of serotonin, dopamine, and oxycontin."
23 Marcel Schwantes, "7 Brutal Truths About Leadership Not Too Many People Want to Hear," *Inc. (June 23, 2020)*. Schwantes is also a speaker, podcaster, and syndicated columnist. www.marcelschwantes.com
24 Sean Kelly, *Becoming Gaia: On the Threshold of Planetary Initiation* (Olympia, WA: Integral Imprint, 2021), 164–165. Kelly is at the California Institute of Integral Studies.

momentum and the confidence that comes from being unscripted, unbought, and uncertain. Our old cultural logic is no longer able to meet the challenges of the moment – challenges that it created.[25]

Practical Way of Working

My discussion of liminal expressions in organizations as spirit, transcendent, totally interconnected, and higher purpose presents these lofty concepts that can contribute to an organization's strategic vision; but what about the mundane, day-to-day details of managing and operating an organization? Peter Vaill described leaders whose spiritual worldview brought them into closer touch with the concrete details of their organizations. Vaill describes his experience of walking through a factory with one of these spiritual leaders:

> Grasping the spirit of a factory permits us to walk through it attending to myriad details, holding multiple simultaneous conversations, asking and answering questions, pausing to be briefed on particular problems, making promises and juggling conflicts, and so on, all the while staying engaged and cheerful about the place. The sense of the spirit of it all is what makes creative immersion in the details possible.[26]

It is not just leaders whose transcendent perspective fosters creative immersion in the details. An employee who develops their liminal consciousness can enhance their sense of when a course of action is the right one and their sense of when it is time to change direction. When writing, if there is a block to a train of thought, there is a

---

25 A. Severan, *Metamodernism and the Return of Transcendence*, vol. 1, Metamodern Spirituality Series, Brendan Graham Dempsey (ed.) (Palimpsest Press, no date), 64. Cited in Joan Walton, *Politics of Knowledge* (Paradigm Explorer, 2022/1). Severan is a lecturer in cultural studies at Queen's College, England.
26 Peter B. Vaill, *Spirited Leading and Learning: Process Wisdom for a New Age* (San Francisco, CA: Jossey-Bass, 1998), 235.

sense that pausing until a different idea flows in is the right thing to do.

Ervin Laszlo calls this liminal awareness a kind of *spontaneous guidance from the universe.* Laszlo says that connecting to the intelligence and wisdom in the universe in an organization doesn't have to be a dramatic event. It can be as easy and simple as being aware of roadblocks and trusting you will receive spontaneous guidance to facilitate doing what you intended to do.[27] In liminal moments, employees and teams can allow their work to unfold around that central inner identity. The process is: be open to guidance from beyond the self, accept the reality of what emerges, sense the importance of the message, and trust the guidance that has been provided.

Reflections on Liminal Organizations

At the beginning of this chapter, I stated that I had a broader understanding of "spirit" and how it is vital in organization and social change. In a transcendent organization there is no tension between material and spiritual pursuits. Wisdom and compassion are integrated in support of human development. Spiritual wisdom and practical economics can become one and the same.[28]

I decided to ask Chat GPT-4 about liminal organizations. This was the response:

> Organizations rooted in liminal consciousness become catalysts for societal progress and positive change. By embracing liminality, organizations shift from a focus on self-interest and profit maximization to one centered on sustainable practices, social responsibility, and ethical decision-making. Liminal organizations

---

[27] Ervin Laszlo, "Timeless Truths & Timely Wisdom: A Conversation with David Lorimer," Institute of Noetic Sciences, 2022. *Italics* added.

[28] Fred Kofman, *The Meaning Revolution: The Power of Transcendent Leadership* (New York: Currency, 2018), 305.

proactively seek out opportunities for environmental stewardship, inclusivity, and community engagement. They invest in research and development, explore disruptive technologies, and embrace agile methodologies to stay ahead of evolving trends. Such organizations recognize their role as a force for good, leveraging their influence and resources to address societal challenges and create a better world.

Artificial intelligence (AI) certainly has a positive and optimistic assessment of liminal organizations. The next section, *Part III – Making the World a Better Place*, suggests how this could unfold.

Part III – Making the World a Better Place

Making the world better is the goal of organization and social change leaders. Whether counseling individuals, leading teams, or facilitating organization and institution change, change leaders use their self and various change methods to influence the direction we are heading, toward a world that is more creative, compassionate, and wise.

In a recent article about "Hope" for a better world, Harry Hutson provides three ways of enacting, embodying, and putting Hope to good use: taking effective action, telling and listening to the truth, and *being* the Hope you want to reside in others.[1]

In this section I encourage change leaders to be the Hope by using imaginal and thoughtful liminal methods in their work to transcend differences and create greater wholeness among individuals, organizations, and societies. Focusing on "being" rather than "doing" will minimize the repetition of the management, policy, and economics strategies that have led to fractures, polarizations, and unsustainable practices.

Chapter 7 – Liminal Methods for Change is about the ways managers, trainers, coaches, consultants, and human resource executives can enhance their current methods of change. Liminal

---

1 Harry Hutson, "The Wisdom of Hope," *Practising Social Change* (Washington, DC: NTL Institute of Applied Behavioral Science, January 2021), 1–7.

methods quiet the active mind until thoughts are transcended and something new is revealed.

Chapter 8 – Transcend Differences. There are many fractures, divisions, differences, and dualities at the root of our existential conflicts. Our racial, gender, sexual orientation, religious, class, ideology, and other identity and cultural differences are particularly challenging for any would-be change leader. This chapter explores how a liminal perspective can positively transcend conflicts about these essential differences in the service of diversity, equity, inclusion, and organization and social change.

Chapter 9 – Create Greater Wholes. We have a reciprocal relationship with the whole biosphere. The Earth is dynamic and creative, becoming more conscious by human intentions and actions.[2] By opening ourselves to a deeply ecological and evolutionary worldview we can create larger organizations and networks that foster global consciousness. Together with nature we create something more – new wholes.

---

2 Jude Currivan, *The Story of Gaia: The Big Breath and the Evolutionary Journey of Our Conscious Planet* (Rochester, NY: Inner Traditions, 2022).

CHAPTER 7

Liminal Methods for Change

> Our contention is that we need to change leaders at their most fundamental level of being – at the level of their consciousness. *Transforming consciousness changes us at the deepest level of our self-identity.* It must always be built on a foundation of principled leadership accompanied by a credible and compelling business case for social responsibility.
>
> Frederick Chavalit Tsao and Chris Laszlo[1]

The contention by Tsao and Laszlo that change is needed at the fundamental level of being – at the level of consciousness – is the way change leaders at every level need to intervene to transform individual, group, organization, industry, institutional, national, and global consciousness. As Tsao and Laszlo also contend, the change must be principled and socially responsible. I would also add ecologically sensitive and responsible to the business case.

There are many change methods that can be enhanced with liminal consciousness. In Chapters 2–6 I have cited some of the major methods:

- Mindfulness and meditation
- Spiritual and religious practices (e.g. prayer and contemplation)

---

1 Frederick Chavalit Tsao and Chris Laszlo, *Quantum Leadership: New Consciousness in Business* (Stanford, CA: Stanford Business Books, 2019), 5.

- Eliminating distractions
- Dreams
- Intention and actively asking for guidance
- Developing the liminal Self
- Connecting inner experience and outer behavior
- Holding tension among differences
- Patience and silence.

There are many sources of information and practices for these methods. All of the methods encourage transformation and self-reflection by cultivating openness and embracing uncertainty. The most popular method in organizations is the practice of mindfulness meditation that navigates the liminal spaces between thoughts, fostering clarity and expanded consciousness.

In this chapter I will focus on methods that can be used by change leaders to create liminal spaces and to go deeper – to the level of self-identity and change of consciousness. They are (1) Training Groups (T-Groups); (2) Coaching; (3) Engagement with Nature; (4) Symbols and Stories; and (5) Embodied Practices. These methods, although at times ambiguous, unsettling, or otherwise challenging to the learner's expectations, are safe and supportive of transformation and growth. Participants can explore their thoughts, ideas, and feelings with freedom to experiment, take risks, and make mistakes. The methods demonstrate that transcendental and spiritual intuition provides valid, authentic, and true information, despite its purely subjective nature.[2]

In my work as an organization development (OD) consultant and trainer, I often brought together managers and their staff to work

---

2 R.W. Hood, "The Construction and Preliminary Validation of a Measure of Reported Mystical Experience," *Journal for the Scientific Study of Religion*, 14:1 (1975), 29.

on a new project in a different location, such as a retreat center. This enabled them to step outside of their everyday routines and focus on organizational issues and projects without distractions. The group processes involved reflection and self-discovery and activities such as journaling, brainstorming, or role-playing. If I had used more of the liminal methods I describe in this chapter, I believe we would have done more to explore values, beliefs, and assumptions and reach a deeper level of change, trust, relationships, and sense of community.

Going Deeper

In 1985, Darya Funches, an NTL Institute colleague, shared a dramatic example of one of her expansions in consciousness. She wrote a seminal article about three gifts that defined her view of effective use of self as an organization development practitioner: the gifts of discernment, presence, and heart.[3] For Funches, these three gifts blended the rational and the intuitive, the integration of the body, mind, emotions, and spirit and the courage to act according to one's beliefs, convictions, knowledge, and feelings. A core message from the insight she shared in "Three Gifts" was that the effective use of self through one's highest levels of consciousness is powerful beyond what practitioners consider their normal tool kits.

In 2022, 37 years later, Funches revealed that progressively higher spiritual consciousness was the source of the three gifts and her insights about them:

> The concept of Three Gifts was an epiphany, a sudden and profound awareness ... I experienced it as a spiritual insight from a higher consciousness. ... The epiphany helped me recognize the power and significance of and requirement for true depth work whenever organizations

---

3 Darya Funches, "Three Gifts of the Organization Development Practitioner," *Organization Development Review*, 54:2 (2022), 4–12. This issue also includes laudatory commentaries on the 1985 article.

> struggle to cure deeply rooted systemic issues. ... What I didn't share at the time was that epiphanies, visions, dreams, and journeys in consciousness have been a fundamental part of my ways of seeing and knowing, being and doing for as long as I can remember.[4]

Funches' revelations about working from higher consciousness are especially inspiring for realizing what is necessary for societal transformation. Doing our own deep work and having the gifts and tools to help others do the same are essential for curing deeply rooted systemic issues.

The psychological paradigm of many change leaders has its roots in materialism. That may begin to change according to Imants Baruss and Julia Mossbridge, members of the American Psychological Association:

> We are in the midst of a sea change. Receding from view is materialism, whereby physical phenomena are assumed to be primary, and consciousness is regarded as secondary. Approaching our sights is a complete reversal of perspective. According to this alternative view, consciousness is primary, and the physical is secondary. In other words, materialism is receding and giving way to ideas about reality in which consciousness plays a key role.[5]

To reverse our perspective from a materialist worldview being primary to a post-materialist worldview that Consciousness is primary, as predicted in the above quote, we will need influential change leaders like Ralph Kilmann to show the way.

During my many years as a trainer and teacher, I used the Thomas–Kilmann Conflict Inventory. In later years, Ralph Kilmann has been interested in using "consciousness-expanding modalities" in

---

4 Darya Funches, "Three Gifts are for Everyone," *Organization Development Review*, 54:2 (2022), 24–25.
5 Imants Baruss and Julia Mossbridge, *Transcendent Mind: Rethinking the Science of Consciousness* (American Psychological Association, 2016).

the workplace to "enhance (and focus) members' commitment, engagement, creativity, and passion on the job." He advocates group and organization training in "self-aware consciousness, ego development, somatic (body) awareness, mindful meditation, gathering and focusing energy fields, mindful yoga to release tensions and stress in the workplace, and spiritual discussions."[6]

Change leaders who introduce liminal methods in their practice will be engaging the whole person as Kilmann requests. They will also become aware of what neuroscience and quantum physics and biology may offer for future system-level possibilities of connection and concern for the well-being of others. Kathryn Pavlovich points out that "at the quantum level, empathy is an entangled, interconnected, and indeterminate shared existence."[7]

Training Groups (T-Groups)

For many years I led or staffed "T-groups" (human interaction groups) for the NTL Institute of Applied Behavioral Science. They were training laboratories (labs) where participants learned interpersonal and group interaction skills such as how to give and receive feedback about their impact on others in the group. The focus was on the "here and now." Participants were encouraged to share their feelings and thoughts about what was happening in the group.

These were not therapy groups. In fact, talking about the past, childhood, or the participant's workplace or home situation was discouraged, since they were not the "here and now." Participants were also not encouraged to share their dreams or any personal issue unless it was affecting their behavior in the group.

---

6 Ralph H. Kilmann, *The Courageous Mosaic: Awakening Society, Systems, and Soul* (Kilmann Diagnostics, 2013).
7 Kathryn Pavlovich, "Introduction to the Special Issue on Quantum Management," *Journal of Management, Spirituality & Religion*, 17:4 (2020), 299–300. Pavlovich is professor of strategic management, entrepreneurship, and sustainability at the University of Waikato, New Zealand.

So how would a training experience that evoked liminal experiences be different from a T-group? Could we call them "L-groups" (liminal groups)?

Participation in a liminal group would be voluntary and would include leaders with clinical experience and access to mental health resources. If liminal methods were introduced to a mandatory group such as a work team, it would start with meditation and stillness. The facilitator would check on the level of comfort of the participants.

The focus would be beyond the "here and now." Dreams would be welcome as information for the group about the messages the members were receiving from Consciousness. Although participants, as in a T-group, would be free to share their observations and feelings about the process of the group, they could also discuss their non-ordinary experiences to help the group gain insight about how non-material reality is manifesting in daily life.

As one person begins to go beyond their ego-identity and is open to whatever comes up from their intuition, the consciousness of the one member is "entangled" with those of the others. Chris Bache, professor emeritus of philosophy and religion at Youngstown State University, says this illustrates the inherent connectivity of life and the powerful tendency of nature to synchronize its many parts into larger wholes. Bache emphasizes that significant group development must recognize the connectivity of consciousness and "the contagious quality of states of awareness."[8]

Takeaways from such a group would be:

- Encouragement to pay attention to the liminal in their daily life and work and their inherent connectedness to others;

- Greater confidence to share these experiences with family and friends;

---

[8] Christopher Bache, "Teaching in the New Paradigm," *Spanda Journal Consciousness & Development 2.0* (2012), 173–179.

- Encouragement to bring the whole person into the workplace.

This expansive view of connectedness between people has implications for the practice of coaching.

Coaching

Coaches provide a comfortable, private, and safe space for clients to explore new possibilities. By being present and attentive and facilitating reflection and self-discovery, they create a sense of trust and confidentiality. A coach can ask questions that trigger the client's memories and curiosity about non-material reality. Asking open-ended questions about recent dreams, vivid memories, and what is happening during periods of silence will expand their worldview, open boundaries that limit curiosity and possibilities, create new mental connections, and expand their life-space. Inquiring about synchronistic events and the metaphors and symbols used by the client can also be helpful.[9]

The questions help the client to move into inquiry and discovery, a place of not knowing, that will evoke Consciousness. For example: (1) What are you doing that feeds your ego instead of the organization? (2) What are you doing that decreases the level of trust others have in you? (3) What unpopular decisions are you avoiding, thus letting others operate without accountability? (4) How are you generating an atmosphere of helplessness by insisting that everything be done according to set procedures? (5) How are you making decisions that support the structure of the organization, not the people?[10]

---

9 My colleague Glenda Eoyang has developed a useful "Power of Questions" for use with individuals or teams (see https://www.hsdinstitute.org/resources/the-power-of-questions.html). *A More Beautiful Question: The Power of Inquiry* by Warren Berger (Bloomsbury USA, 2016) also has suggestions to spark breakthrough ideas.

10 For readers who are fans of psychological archetypes, these are the archetypes present in the five questions: (1) Negative King/Queen; (2) Evil Witch/Wizard; (3) Abdicating King/Queen; (4) Wounded King/Queen; (5) Dominating Warrior/Amazon.

Jungian analyst Jean Bolen describes liminal consciousness as an emotional field that is generated between her and her clients that affects how she relates to the client, for example, whether to be involved with the client's issues or to be more detached.[11]

Molly Worthen writes about spiritual coaches who evoke unseen forces in the universe, especially the divine feminine, "to counter the machismo that dominates American entrepreneurial culture." She quotes an interviewee: "Part of it is strategy [to make money], but I come more from the point of view of consciousness – what wants to be birthed through me – versus a more capitalistic, masculine approach to business."[12]

Worthen's evocation of the divine feminine also suggests other orientations for coaches who are willing to evoke archetypal forces to deal with other systemic social justice issues such as deep ecology.

Engagement with Nature

My grandparents, Hans and Margaret Halsrud, immigrated from Norway and settled on a farm in Minnesota. I enjoyed my summers there, in their gardens, among the trees, and with the horses and pigs. I later learned the Norwegian saying "Ut på tur, aldri sur" – "out on hike, never in a bad mood" – which means you never regret going outside.

We can let nature induce liminal experiences that transcend our ego by simply walking around the block and purposely connecting with nature with all of the senses. Business psychologist Terence Sexton says, "While sitting in nature in silence, if you ask nature a question while in this quiet state, an answer may come to you."[13] He adds:

---

11 Jean S. Bolen, *Goddesses in Everywoman: A New Psychology of Women* (San Francisco, CA: Harper and Row, 1984).

12 Molly Worthen, "Witches. Today, They Can Be Your Coach," *New York Times* (June 3, 2022). Dr. Worthen is a historian at the University of North Carolina at Chapel Hill who writes about America's religious culture.

13 Terence Sexton, *Consciousness Beyond Consumerism: A Psychological Path to Sustainability* (Ashford, Kent, U.K.: Aqumens Publishing, 2021), 235–236.

> Does nature really speak to us? ... If we assume we are an intrinsic part of nature, then it does not matter ... If we are all connected through [Consciousness], then our intuition and nature's voice are the same.[14]

If we agree with Sexton's observation that our intuition and nature's voice are the same, perhaps our work in organization and societal change should explicitly include nature's voice. If we listen to nature, our routines will likely be disrupted. We may stop eating our usual foods. We may get away from the noise of our surroundings. We might begin to see different people and think new thoughts. We may even reduce our access to technology and heed the warnings about artificial intelligence (AI) and its recent manifestations in Chat GPT and Bard (See 'Appendix – Is Artificial Intelligence Sentient?').

Symbols and Stories

Symbols and stories are used to define and capture the essential truths about an organization. They give the leaders and members of the organization a context of meaning that impels and justifies their actions.[15] Stories about management philosophy may become normative prescriptions. I remember the story about the founder of Marriott taking coffee to the loading dock workers early in the morning. New members of the organization ignore these stories and the symbolic lessons they contain at their peril.

Symbols. All symbols (such as a tree, water, a cross, etc.) can open a liminal space. We encounter these symbols in dreams and during lucid waking moments. Historically objects of significance, called talismans, were imbued with a specific power by their wearer to serve specific purposes – for example, carrying a rabbit's foot for good luck. The nature of the talisman is not as important as the

---

14 Ibid., 236.
15 Edwin E. Olson, "Using imagery and symbols in organization change," *OD Practitioner*, 37:3 (2005), 23–28.

intention of its bearer. For a time, in recognition of my Viking heritage, I carried a miniature Thor's hammer.

Sacred sites such as Stonehenge in England, Iona in Scotland, Lady of Lourdes in France, and countless non-Western sites are larger and more dramatic symbols that are regarded as repositories of wisdom, energy, illumination, and healing. As portals to Consciousness, sacred sites in nature such as mountains can evoke a sense of the Earth's unified consciousness – the living, the dead, our diverse cultures, and the material and spiritual worlds.[16]

Stories. The poems and stories from religious writings and Indigenous knowledge applied to a specific situation thousands of years ago, but they are relevant today because the patterns and immutable problems they reveal are universal.

The great sages of history used parables and stories to let their listeners think for themselves, draw their own conclusions, and do the right thing. Moral consciousness emerges in response to exposure to a stimulus like a parable that challenges conventional wisdom and disorients the listener to see things differently. The chaos that is created allows a shift in perspective and a sense that something is greater than our self-interest.[17]

Telling and listening to stories invites other stories from our life experience to emerge. Stories energize and illuminate what we have forgotten, what is possible, and what the universe wants us to know. Stories foster self-identification and allow more connections with others.

Culture change leaders can intervene in the organization by identifying symbols and stories of what is trying to emerge. Rather

---

16 A mountain peak near Las Vegas, known as Avi Kwa Ame or Spirit Mountain, is the sacred creation site for Yuman-speaking Native Americans. It may soon become a national monument.

17 See Edwin E. Olson, "Ethical Decision-Making and Metaphors: Enhancing Moral Consciousness Using Parables and Complexity Theory," in Andrew Tait and Kurt A. Richardson (eds), *Moving Forward with Complexity* (Emergent Publications, 2011), 331–347.

than a frontal attack on the organizational norms, raising liminal consciousness with symbols and stories will gradually identify ways to deviate from the given and the usual. This will also reduce the danger of believing only a single story.

Embodied Practices

Rick Rubin, a legendary music producer, has lessons for change leaders in all fields. He creates music by asking his clients to pay attention to the energy in the universe that is resonating at a particular moment. He says the energy Source is "a wisdom surrounding us, an inexhaustible offering that is always available." Tiny fragments of the vastness of Source are also stored within us. Our task is to be present with and accept "what is happening in the eternal now."[18]

This energy is embodied and expressed in art, music, sound, and dance. Creative artists, musicians, and dancers reach for this Source by releasing attachment to their perceived self and its limitations. They expand to their liminal Self. Rubin says "As artists, we are on a continual quest to get closer to the universe by getting closer to Self, moving ever nearer to the point where we can no longer tell where one begins and the other ends. We're on a distant metaphysical journey from the here to the now."[19]

Change leaders in organizations can use drawing, painting, music, and movement to foster liminal consciousness and create new patterns of thinking, doing, and creating. Participants in my workshops have created mandalas to see patterns of relationships in their organization. I have found that constructing anything within a circle radiates a relaxing, meditative, and healing energy.

Music is also useful to create liminal experiences. As discussed in *Chapter 2 – Experiencing Betwixt and Between*, everything in the universe is in a constant state of vibration. Introducing soothing

---

18 Rick Rubin, *The Creative Act: A Way of Being* (New York: Penguin Press, 2023).
19 Ibid., 258–259.

and harmonious music at the beginning of a human development workshop affects the participants on mental, physical, and spiritual levels. Participant movement in a workshop can also be a portal to self-discovery, connectedness, and deep knowing.

New Methodological Boundaries

If we are willing to engage with liminal consciousness and use the kind of methods described in this chapter, we can transcend our current level of self-actualization. The methods I have discussed so far are all capable of inducing a liminal state in which you are absorbed in what you are doing. Time seems to fall away, and you are flowing into the experience itself.[20] The core idea is to make the time and space to listen. Business consultants Perry Marshall and John Fancher explicitly tell their clients that the universe is telling them what they need to be doing. They say, "Your to-do list can wait. In fact, the universe knows what your to-do list *should* be. And if you are not listening, you will not be doing the right things."[21]

For those who wish to go deeper into experiencing psychic phenomena (psi), there are many reputable mediums that can aid in perceiving spirits and intuitive messages. Mark Anthony, a medium with whom I have had a personal positive experience, says the key to learning these mystical abilities is "to *recognize* the presence of spirits and the signs they present, *accepting* the reality of the contact, *feeling* the importance and emotional significance of the message, and *trusting* your feelings as well as truth and guidance provided by the message. Recognize, accept, feel, trust (RAFT)."[22]

---

20 For other ideas to think deeply see Johann Hari, *Stolen Focus: Why You Can't Pay Attention – and How to Think Deeply Again* (New York: Crown, 2022), 57.
21 Perry Marshall and John Fancher, *Memos from the Head Office: Channeling the Muse in Business and in Life* (Perry Marshall & Associates, 2021), 121.
22 Mark Anthony, *The Afterlife Frequency: The Scientific Proof of Spiritual Contact and How That Awareness Will Change Your Life* (Novato, CA: New World Library, 2021), 76.

Sandra Ingerman, a teacher of shamanism, provides a guide for anyone who wishes to learn the practice of shamanic journeying. In her spiritual journey, Ingerman encountered helping spirits and learned about a "true definition of power" using "our energy to create transformation for ourselves, others and the planet."[23] She says that shamanism teaches us that everything that exists is alive and has a spirit, and that we are joined with the Earth and all of life via our spiritual interconnectedness. In a shamanic journey, a person learns how to communicate with the spirit of the trees, plants, animals, insects, birds, fish, reptiles, and rocks, as well as the spirit of the elements of earth, air, water, and fire. They directly experience the web of life.[24]

From a scientific perspective, the shamanic journey occurs in a field of quantum connections and is not restricted by space-time constraints.[25]

A New Skunk Works?

This may be a time for a new formulation of "skunk works" for organizations.[26] Organizations could set up experimental groups to

---

23 From Sandra Ingerman, *Shamanic Journeying* (Boulder, CO: Sounds True, 2004), 2–3.
24 Ibid., 8. Maria Rodale in *Love, Nature, Magic: Shamanic Journeys into the Heart of My Garden* (Chelsea Green Publishing, 2023) shares her conversations with the spirits of plants and animals, each of whom has its own message to her personally and to humanity.
25 Ede Frecska, Mihály Hoppál, and Luis E. Luna, "Non-locality and the Shamanic State of Consciousness," *NeuroQuantology*, 14:2 (June 2016), 155–165.
26 The term originated during the Second World War with Lockheed's Advanced Development Projects Division in Burbank, California. A closely guarded incubator was set up in a circus tent next to a plastics factory. The strong smells that wafted into the tent made the Lockheed R&D workers think of the foul-smelling "Skonk Works" factory in Al Capp's *Li'l Abner* comic strip. The term has become generalized to apply to high-priority R&D projects in large organizations which feature a small elite team removed from the normal working environment and given freedom from management constraints. Examples are Google X Lab, Microsoft Research, special teams at Boeing, and the lab established by Steve Jobs to develop the Macintosh computer. The

do liminal work and see what emerges. The group would meet each other as authentic Selves and experience transpersonal intimacy and spiritual partnerships. If everyone is in an enlightened space, they will think anew about what is possible and learn to think about the unthinkable.

In positive psychology terms, the group would be in a flow state.[27] The group would be fully immersed in their purpose, fully involved, and enjoying the process. The members would be centered in their consciousness and allow their work to unfold around their liminal Selves. The group could open up new ways to solve problems and unstick fossilized worldviews. The group could be advertised as a "learning laboratory" or "learning community," methods used successfully by the NTL Institute for 75 years. Such groups combine research and education, and develop actions to guide the future.

A major challenge facing those who would like to make the world better is resolving the illusory dualities and unresolved differences in our organizations and society. I explore how liminal consciousness could help transcend those differences in the next chapter.

expectations for the products developed by skunk works have changed in the twenty-first century from "something that makes their competitors say 'Wow'" to "something that makes their competitors' customers say 'Wow.'" Rather than sequestering skunk works, the companies now tend to promote communication between them and marketing, design, and accounting departments.

27 Mihaly Csikszentmihalyi, *Flow: The Psychology of Optimal Experience* (New York: Harper, 2008).

CHAPTER 8

Transcend Differences

> When the opposites are realized to be one, discord melts into concord, battles become dances, and old enemies become lovers. We are then in a position to make friends with all of our universe, not just one half of it.
>
> Ken Wilbur[1]

The tension in society stemming from our multiple crises of the pandemic, economic and political instability, global climate collapse, culture wars, and racism has led to prolonged periods of pain, loss, and possible system breakdowns. The unresolved tension has created divisions and fractures in society. If we can transcend differences, we can connect on a deeper level, create a more inclusive society, and live more peacefully and harmoniously. Transcending differences reveals our shared humanity, our commonality with other cultures, and our capacity to be accepting of others.

In this chapter I explore (1) the polarities and duality thinking about differences; (2) the resulting cultural and social fragmentation; and (3) how liminal consciousness shows that the opposites are one and how discord can melt into concord as Ken Wilbur envisions.

---

1 Ken Wilbur, *No Boundaries: Eastern and Western Approaches to Personal Growth* (Boston, MA: Shambala Publications, 1979), 29.

CHAPTER 8

Polarities and Dualistic Thinking

Most everything we experience has an opposite – light/dark, breathe in/breathe out, black/white, pleasant/unpleasant, awake/asleep. These are seeming dualities. For example, when we say "that rose smells wonderful," we separate the rose from its odor, but we intuitively know they are connected. We create a distinction, a duality that simplifies and identifies significant differences.[2]

If we remain unaware that these dualities are essentially illusory, we will be stuck in dualistic and polarized thinking, a win/lose mentality of us versus them. The dualistic mind is binary, either/or thinking. It only knows by comparison, opposition, and differentiation. "The polarized mind is the fixation on a single point of view to the utter exclusion of competing points of view."[3] It uses words like good/evil, pretty/ugly, and smart/stupid without recognizing the many degrees of difference between the two ends of each polarity. Gregory Blann, a Dervish sheikh and author, urges us to not think in terms of good and bad. If we think of experiences being either bitter or sweet, we are more likely to see the interconnectedness of life. "The more holistic our view becomes beyond limited labels of good and bad, the more our compassion for others can flow."[4]

It is in the conflict that both individuals and groups are able to learn and grow if they see the underlying wholeness of the dualities. When we divide reality into two, we create experiences of otherness and division, but reality, the totality of human existence, is one and unified at deeper orders of reality.

To truly resolve difference, the parties in conflict need to see each other as part of an evolution of a both/and world of infinite

---

2 Thanks to Mauro Berganzi for this understanding of duality and non-duality. The Peri Center webinar with Shantena Sabadini, March 6, 2022.
3 Kirk J. Schneider, "Today's Biggest Threat: The Polarized Mind," *Scientific American* (2020).
4 Gregory Blann, *When the Oceans Merge: The Contemporary Sufi and Hasidic Teachings of Pir Vilayat Inayat Khan and Rabbi Zalman Schachter-Shalomi*, 217 (Rhinebeck, NY: Monkfish Publishing, 2019).

possibilities. Our differences are clues to a both/and solution, a oneness.⁵ The apparent dualities are necessary manifestations of the whole.

Cultural and Social Fragmentation

The fragmentation, splits, and polarities in global culture and politics are more obvious and greater now than ever before in living memory. Trust in governments, business, and the media around the world is also collapsing, especially in democracies. Wars have brought many democracies together, but the threat of left–right polarizations remains. There has been an increase in centralized digital power, surveillance, and control. Many do not think they are being told the truth.⁶

Psychotherapist Carolyn Baker believes that our cultural separation stems from our inability to be "present" and authentically "see" those with an opposing worldview, or to "allow them to authentically see us even when they don't see what we see." Instead of blaming, cursing, shaming, or shunning those who do not see what we see, we could try and see "their deep wounds, their vulnerability, their terror of things they don't understand, and the toll that separation has taken on them."⁷

Our social fragmentation is not just in our political parties, but in our companies, professional associations, colleges and universities, school boards, neighborhoods, and families. Jeffrey Kripal says, "How can we deny humanity to someone simply because he or she has a different color of skin, or holds a different set of beliefs

---

5 *Vedanta* and its great teachers have illuminated a path that guides us to the place where it is possible to live fully in this relative world, with full remembrance of oneness. *Vedanta* gives us a vision of 200% of life.
6 Edelman's 2022 global *Trust Barometer*, a survey of 35,000 respondents in 28 countries.
7 Carolyn Baker, *Undaunted: Living Fiercely into Climate Meltdown in an Authoritarian World* (Hannacroix, NY: Apocryphile Press, 2022), 32. Baker is also a life coach and spiritual counselor.

in her or his head?" Once we realize this, "We will stop enacting these petty bigotries in our politics and societies. They will become unthinkable, impossible."[8]

While writing this chapter, I had the following dream of the interaction among a group of white people about a Christmas card:

> A man (me) held up a Christmas card that said, "I hope that Santa gets out of the hospital so we can have a white Christmas." There is some booing in the crowd. Although all of the graphics on the card showed a snowy Christmas scene, some people saw this as an example of white supremacy. They could not support those who saw it as a winter scene with snow.

The card in the dream was nonsensical; it said that Santa had some influence over whether it would snow on Christmas. However, a conflict ensued over whether wanting a "white" Christmas was racist.

At first, I thought the dream was pointing to the need for creative solutions about how white people think about symbols of racism, but then I realized that the conflict over semantics and political correctness was distracting the whites from the realities and consequences of racism and colorism that inflict untold suffering and oppression. It was a powerful message from Consciousness that whites need to transcend their fears of losing face and being shamed and work to eliminate racial practices rather than be distracted by potential symbols of racism.

In her book on white fragility, Robin Diangelo points out that white progressives can be the most difficult for people of color because "to the degree that we think we have arrived, we will put our energy into making sure that others see us as having arrived."[9]

---

[8] Jeffrey Kripal, *The Flip: Epiphanies of Mind and the Future of Knowledge* (New York: Bellevue Literary Press, 2019), 184.

[9] Robin Diangelo, *White Fragility: Why It's So Hard for White People to Talk About Racism* (Boston, MA: Beacon Press, 2018), 5.

White progressive energy needs to go into "engaging in ongoing self-awareness, continuing education, relationship building, and actual antiracist practices."[10]

How Liminal Consciousness Can Help

Liminal consciousness is an antidote for the fragmentation and oppression in our societies that stems from the materialist worldview and a zero-sum mentality that progress for "them" must come at the expense of "us."[11] The resolution of polarities, differences, and fragmentations is possible because of the fundamental force of love in the universe, the force of attraction that brings things together. The tension between opposites and polarities is transcended as a new reality emerges and integrates disparities, revealing the wholeness of reality.

How we currently make meaning and examine existing assumptions is mostly within the materialist paradigm. Transcending our current polarization requires our liminal imagination and wisdom. My colleague Kate Cowie uses storytelling in her work to harness the power of our imagination to make sense of the world; "seemingly disconnected things cohere; truths which were hidden are revealed; and answers to our questions become clear."[12]

Rather than focusing on eliminating the discomfort, reflect on conflict as an opportunity to move beyond constraints that prevent learning and innovating. Intuitive, liminal thinking beyond dualities allows warring parties to move beyond ego, individual and group identities, the desire for power and control, and public posturing. Instead of "either/or," a "both/and" state of mind enables us to hold both positions simultaneously without conflict.[13]

---

10 Ibid.
11 Heather McGhee, *Sum of Us: What Racism Costs Everyone and How We Can Progress Together* (One World, 2021).
12 Kate Cowie, *Finding Merlin* (London: Marshall Cavendish, 2012), xv.
13 Terence Sexton, *Consciousness Beyond Consumerism: A Psychological Path to Sustainability* (Ashford, Kent, U.K.: Aqumens Publishing, 2021), 211.

When we transcend differences, we are living holistically. We see new possibilities. If we are fully aware of our connection to a transcendent reality, we will expect to experience synchronistic events and anticipate receiving images and messages that point to a deeper understanding and wisdom,[14] and even to an alternative future.

When an individual experiences prolonged conflict, they need to be open to letting go of an attachment to a position and allowing something from liminal consciousness to emerge. Letting go of what we think is "right" and opening to a new understanding transcends the differences.

When the ego insists that you maintain your position, think of it as a clue that you need to let go. It is useful to ask questions such as: "What am I telling myself? How true is it?" "Is there another way of seeing that?" Be aware of your impulse to act, then wait for a vision from your liminal Self. Without access to a deeper wisdom, we risk a poverty of imagination and may act out of short-term self-interest without concern for the common good.[15]

From the liminal perspective of non-duality, we see how we are cooperative and caring. We no longer have to compartmentalize business and personal, mind and body, spiritual and material, and attempt to balance the parts. We experience our lives as integrated in a coherent, rich, harmonious whole.[16]

Despite all the tensions and problems that arise, we can see that

---

[14] Inspired by Chris Laszlo, "Prospective Theorizing: Researching for Social Impact," *Journal of Management, Spirituality & Religion*, 18:6 (2021), 19–34.

[15] I must pay homage to Dr. James Klonoski, my political science professor at St. Olaf College. He instilled in me the concept of the "public interest" which was reinforced as we read John Kenneth Galbraith's *The Affluent Society* and surveyed the opinions of the citizens of Northfield, Minnesota about whether we were "starving the public sector." To help with the interviews, my future wife Judith drove me around the town in her mother's car. That should have been a clue about what life with me would be like.

[16] Adapted from Dianne Collins, *Do You QuantumThink?* (New York: Select Books, 2011), 113.

differences and dualities contribute to a diverse and flourishing democratic society. Our unique personal and group identities and our diverse social and cultural practices are essential for creating what's new, what's next, what's needed.[17] Liminal consciousness acknowledges and values diverse perspectives. It fosters a culture of inclusivity and collaboration where individuals feel safe expressing their ideas. Diverse voices are heard and valued, driving innovation and social progress. Diversity can also increase productivity, reduce employee turnover, connect to a wider range of consumers, and increase revenue.[18]

Living in oneness is to live in joy and bliss, where there is no past or future, only now, a place of endless peace, harmony, and unconditional love. Unfortunately, we can never imagine it fully. To understand or experience anything, we need to compare it to something else, which immediately brings us into duality. Oneness by definition is incomparable.

We can only attain oneness by transcending opposites. Fortunately, there is a global movement toward greater moral oneness that is led, in many places, by the younger generation and supported by the wisdom of elders.[19] I explore this in the next chapter.

---

[17] Tom Atlee, "Engaging with the Evolving Whole," blog, *Tom Atlee's Transformational Thinkpad* (January 31, 2022).
[18] McKinsey.com
[19] Elena Mustakova, *Global Unitive Healing: Integral Skills for Personal and Collective Transformation* (Light on Light Press, 2021), 190.

CHAPTER 9

Create Greater Wholes

As individuals, groups, organizations, and institutions develop a liminal consciousness, I believe we will progress to a more just and peaceful world. But will the progress be fast enough? Do we have time for our collective consciousness to evolve naturally? Terence Sexton says it would be too late to ensure the survival of humans and much of our biodiversity.[1] Our looming existential crises need immediate attention.

If greater wholes, networks, and international alliances are formed by individuals and organizations with liminal consciousness, we would have reason to choose Hope. With their combined resources and wisdom, they could influence governmental and political leaders and create a tipping point. Coherent, synergistic wholes can resolve our divisions, dichotomies, and dualisms and manage new complexities, as life on the planet has been doing for billions of years.

Think of the world as a global learning community with unique ways of living and being. The whole we create can reflect the diverse cultures from a stance of equality. We can learn what gives vitality to each culture.[2]

---

1 Terence Sexton, *Consciousness Beyond Consumerism: A Psychological Path to Sustainability* (Ashford, Kent, U.K.: Aqumens Publishing, 2021), 286.
2 Sangeeta Parameshwar, Param Srikantia, and Jessica Heineman-Pieper, "Poverty Alleviation at an International Development Organization: Resurrecting the Human Being as Subject," *Vikalpa*, 34:2 (April–June, 2009), 1.

Toward Greater Wholes

What could create greater wholes? Theologian Ilia Delio argues that greater wholes are continually being created in our evolutionary human experience of consciousness. We can choose to have the "capacity for greater wholeness."[3]

Each new whole, whether it is a new business venture, association, or alliance, becomes connected to a universal field of energy and information that expands our systems view and capability of action from a broader context.[4] Liminal consciousness reveals insights about the self, family, community, and society that becomes the ground of a new path in our lives and careers.[5] The more places, events, persons, animals, and plants in which we experience Consciousness, the greater the range of our human consciousness.

Wholeness includes unity and diversity, separateness and interconnection, harmony and disturbance, the individual and the collective, and every other polarity we can think of. It is through the generative interactions between or among those differences that we are able to bring forth the wisdom and resourcefulness of the new greater whole.[6] The challenge for the parts of the whole (leaders, teams, and organizations) is to include all of the relevant parts of the greater whole?[7] They need to ask, "Who else should be part of this?" "What else do we need to know or learn?" "What is possible now?"

---

3 Ilia Delio, *The Hours of the Universe: Reflections on God, Science, and the Human Journey* (Maryknoll, NY: Orbis Books, 2021), 229.
4 Ibid.
5 Thanks to Mike Morrell, the collaborating editor with Richard Rohr of *The Divine Dance: The Trinity and Your Transformation*. Mike curates contemplative and community experiences for persons who wish to develop their own mystical path. He "takes joy in holding space for the extraordinary transformation that can take place at the intersection of anticipation, imagination, and radical acceptance." Mikemorrell.org
6 Ibid.
7 From Tom Atlee, "Engaging with the Evolving Whole," blog, *Tom Atlee's Transformational Thinkpad* (January 31, 2022).

When you have the intuition that someone is going to telephone you, and in fact they do, you can call it a coincidence, but think of the electromagnetic fields that surround you as a multidimensional holographic field of living intelligence, energy, and connection. Our thoughts, feelings, and desires are in the middle of this field. We are connected to all that matters, to everything we need, to a new story. Dianne Collins eloquently summarizes the implications of this essential connectedness:

> everything on Earth exists as one interconnected whole. ... [W]e are intrinsically, intimately, undeniably connected physically as well as through the energetic, mind, and spiritual dimensions. What does all this mean? Our own nature is singular, expansive, and unbounded. The quantum paradox is, we experience and express an individual mind and collective mind simultaneously, yet at our core consciousness we are one. We could say we are "quantumly entangled."[8]

Creating greater wholes is a progressive process of transcendence of the limits of our understanding and appreciation that goes beyond ordinary, everyday life. These greater institutional and organizational wholes will manifest greater inclusiveness, equity, and cooperation.

Presence

Peter Senge and his colleagues popularized the idea of "presence," an awareness of the larger whole, leading to actions that can help to shape its evolution and our future.[9] They point out that the whole is unfolding within each of us, within the present situation:

> Serving the emerging whole means paying attention to what's right here within my awareness, what's completely

---

8 Dianne Collins, *Do You QuantumThink?* (New York: Select Books, 2011), 111.
9 Peter M. Senge, C. Otto Scharmer, Joseph Jaworski, and Betty Sue Flowers, *Presence: An Exploration of Profound Change in People, Organizations, and Society* (New York: The Crown Publishing Group, 2004).

local, and surrendering to what's being asked of me now. The deepest systems we enact are woven into the fabric of everyday life, down to the most minute detail.

Whatever goals a leader may have for changing their organization, they can experience the whole that is unfolding in the present. They then can use their liminal Selves as instruments for something larger to emerge.[10] Senge says waking up to who we really are is to link with and act from our highest future Self. This Self can bring forth new worlds. "It's the point where the fire of creation burns and enters the world through us."[11]

The Wholeness of the Earth

Einstein said our experience of being separate from the whole is an optical delusion of our consciousness. This delusion is a kind of prison that restricts us to our personal desires and to affection for a few persons nearest to us. We can free ourselves from this prison by widening our circle of compassion to embrace all living creatures and the whole of nature in its beauty.[12]

For Einstein, the greater whole includes the Earth and all of its inhabitants. Integrating environmental sustainability to a corporate business model should include "creating a more flourishing world, a place where people everywhere live in healthy communities, prosper, and can live life to the fullest."[13] Reducing a carbon footprint is a worthy goal, but a positive impact needs to include "increasing economic prosperity while contributing to a healthy regenerative natural environment and improving human well-being."[14]

---

10 Ibid., 234–235.
11 Ibid., 240.
12 Albert Einstein and Leopold Infeld, *The Evolution of Physics* (Touchstone, 1967), 136.
13 Ignacio Perez, Lori D. Kendall, and Chris Laszlo, "Positive-Impact Companies: Toward a New Paradigm of Value Creation," *Organizational Dynamics*, 50 (2021), 1–11.
14 Ibid.

"Climate change" is a weak term for what Jonathan Rowson, director of Perspectiva and former director of the Social Brain Centre at the Royal Society of Arts, says is a "systemic climate collapse." "Collapse," not "change," because our lungs collapse, financial systems collapse, and we collapse in exhaustion at the end of a difficult day.[15]

How do we create not only a sustainable but a life-enhancing culture? Psychotherapist Carolyn Baker hopes that we will receive grace if we accept the reality of humanity's predicament and engage in the inner and outer work that is needed to face that reality.[16] As I have argued in this book, I believe that the grace that Baker envisions is the intrusion of Consciousness into our human condition.

Technology Wholes

In 2016 Kevin Kelly, founding editor of *Wired* magazine, described the hopeful consequences of the exponential growth of technology as a cloud of machine intelligence, linking billions of human minds in a single supermind of unimagined complexity that provides a new way of thinking and a new mind for our species.[17] How has that worked out? Our new state of Internet connectedness, with all of its benefits, could also sink humanity into an era of meaninglessness without the deeper wisdom of Consciousness.

Philosopher Pieter Lemmens has taken Kelly's analysis further and describes how the *technosphere* interacts with both the biosphere and the *noosphere*, the increasingly impactful layer of thought (*nous*) surrounding the Earth since the birth of scientific reason.[18] He points out that technology is not just embedded in Earth's ecology

---

15 Jonathan Rowson, "Integrating Our Souls, Systems, and Society," *On Being with Krista Tippett* (July 18, 2019).
16 Carolyn Baker, *Undaunted: Living Fiercely into Climate Meltdown in an Authoritarian World* (Hannacroix, NY: Apocryphile Press, 2022), 183.
17 Kevin Kelly, *The Inevitable: Understanding the 12 Technological Forces That Will Shape Our Future* (New York: Penguin Publishing Group, 2016), 291–292.
18 Pieter Lemmens, "Thinking Technology Big Again: Reconsidering the Question of the Transcendental and 'Technology with a Capital T' in the Light of the Anthropocene," *Found Sci* 27 (2022), 171–187. https://doi.org/10.1007/

anymore but is increasingly becoming its prime animating factor. The future habitability of the Earth is becoming a technological question.[19]

> It is on the future development of this planetary techno-noosphere that the future of the biosphere now crucially depends, the fate of the one determining the fate of the other. ... The future survival of humanity requires a fundamental reframing of this techno-noosphere.[20]

Lemmens emphasizes that we must reframe the techno-noosphere. The reframing must go beyond Western naturalism, which conceives of the world as a giant standing reserve; Lemmens insists we include non-Western Indigenous ways of technical world-making such as animist, totemist, analogist ontologies that are totally different.[21] These ways of making sense use liminal consciousness.

Technology can lead to new wholes, but whatever form they take, liminal consciousness must inform the next stage of their evolution.

A Wholeness Narrative

Our historic, ethnic, and cultural worldviews need to be transcended by a narrative that combines the best of what our sciences and wisdom traditions can offer.

The Narrative: We are spirit-infused beings in a world that is alive with meaning. We are not separate self-absorbed individuals, we are cooperative, caring, and compassionate. We are not driven only to compete ("survival of the fittest"), we also pursue flourishing ("living

---

s10699-020-09732-7. Lemmens is at the Institute for Science in Society, Radboud University Nijmegen, Nijmegen, Netherlands.
19 Lemmens calls for a dialogue between philosophy of technology, Earth system science (ESS), Gaia theory, cybernetics, and the sciences of thermodynamics.
20 Ibid.
21 Shoshana Zuboff, *The Age of Surveillance Capitalism: The Fight for a Human Future at the New Frontier of Power* (Public Affairs, 2019).

life to its fullest"). We do not see nature as an external resource for consumption. We are an integral part of it. We continually revise our science-based assumptions about what it means to be human and the nature of community and organizational life.

Complexity quantum science has given us new ways to theorize about how to tackle wicked problems such as climate change and social justice. Our interconnectedness fosters cooperation for the common good. The new systems we create have permeable and expanding boundaries that include difference and new connected networks. These dynamic relationships are constantly moving, responding to the underlying forces of and connections to Consciousness, and creating unity in the diversity of the world.[22]

After this theorizing about a new narrative, let's look at some specific greater wholes that draw from such a narrative and are making a difference.

New Global Wholes[23]

New systems to promote global wholeness can bring experts about systems thinking, ecological interconnectedness, spiritually inspired ethics, complexity science – including people speaking for nature, for future generations, and from the habitually ignored margins of society and life. The more often we successfully develop a more expansive worldview, the more possible its vision becomes in the

---

22 This narrative has been inspired by Ilia Delio (theologian), Chris Laszlo (organization theorist), and Ruth Kastner and Gary Goldberg (quantum scientists): Ilia Delio, *The Unbearable Wholeness of Being: God, Evolution, and the Power of Love* (Marymount, NJ: Orbis Books, 2013), 202; Chris Laszlo, "Prospective Theorizing: Researching for Social Impact," *Journal of Management, Spirituality & Religion*, 18:6 (2021), 19–34; Ruth E. Kastner and Gary Goldberg, "Connecting the Actuality of Things in Space – Time to the Reality of Possibility in Quantumland," Peri Center (February 19, 2022).
23 In creating new wholes, the challenge is to be globally inclusive in the drafting and adoption of any new international norms. Currently, the only world constitution is the United Nations Charter, which lays out a rules-based international order.

real, everyday world of evolving greater wholeness.[24] I regularly participate in the offerings of the following seven organizations.

Holos Project Earth

Holos Project Earth is a gathering space for leading-edge holistic thinkers and practitioners building an international network, capable of and committed to changing the discourse and practice of leadership and governance in the face of the meta-crisis of global challenges humanity faces today. The Project explores how to shift thinking and practice to a holistic perspective to better address the complex challenges of the twenty-first century. The group is committed to discovering how to personally live a holistic life to assist with the process of building self-organizing communities of practice engaged in applying the holistic perspective. I have participated in the webinars sponsored by the Holos Project. Dr. Claudius van Wyk is founder and chair of the Holos Earth Project.

https://holos-earth.org

Institute of Noetic Sciences (IONS)

The mission of the Institute of Noetic Sciences is to reveal the interconnected nature of reality through scientific exploration and personal discovery. As scientists focus on what are common but not often understood phenomena, they are also aware of the vast historical records of wisdom practices that also speak to the mysteries and possibilities which allow us to access more of our human capacities. The IONS scientists apply the rigors of their respective disciplines to explore such phenomena, with a focus on understanding humanity's inherent interconnectedness and the inner wisdom common to us all. They envision the creation of a more compassionate and thriving world. I have attended the weekly

---

24 From Tom Atlee, "Engaging with the Evolving Whole," blog, *Tom Atlee's Transformational Thinkpad* (January 31, 2022).

webinars sponsored by IONS and have enrolled in one of their courses by Dr. Helané Wahbeh.

https://noetic.org/

Manifest Nirvana

Manifest Nirvana "is a virtual haven for *integral spiritual practice*, where sovereign souls, radical spirits, and integral pioneers will find their home. But it is also a future vision for the evolution of humanity – a utopian ideal for those still bold enough to dream big." This statement by Andrew Cohen, the founder and leader of the organization, characterizes the spirit in which its various offerings are conducted. I have attended several of the teaching sessions. In *Chapter 5 – Teams*, I have described a group process used in one of the sessions.

https://www.manifest-nirvana.com/

One Mountain

One Mountain is a weekly, interactive, online broadcast that includes rich, spiritually activating, transformational content, group prayer, and encouragement to live love as religion. I have attended many of the inspirational webinars presented by Dr. Marc Gafni.

https://www.onemountainmanypaths.org/

EARTHwise Centre

The goal of the Centre is to make civilizational transformation feasible by purposefully connecting human potential with evolutionary systems design, collective intelligence, transformative technologies, and regenerative business models. They operate as a worldwide educational, training, coaching, research, publication, and leadership center for developing the necessary capacities, systems, governance, tools, and pathways for a planetary civilization, offering integral systemic support and services for individuals, groups, teams, organizations, communities, networks, and governments. The Centre serves as the host and steward for the EARTHwise Constitution and their Partnership Alliance for a Planetary Civilization. The Centre also serves as host and publisher for the *Future Humans Trilogy* and its projects and courses. Their services and projects support the implementation of the UN Sustainable Development Goals (SDGs), while taking this further to lead for whole systems change, and the transformation of the human condition of our sustainability crisis. I have attended several of the workshops presented by founder Dr. Anneloes Smitsman and her co-author Dr. Jean Houston.

https://www.earthwisecentre.org

The Shift Network

The Shift Network's vision is to empower a global network of evolutionary change agents through media, education, and resources featuring leading wisdom keepers and visionaries. They provide a platform for an emerging culture to connect, collaborate, and co-create. They have served over 3,200,000 people, with customers in 180 countries. They have featured over 3,100 thought leaders in domains as diverse as spirituality, holistic health, psychology, Qigong, somatics, Indigenous wisdom, enlightened business, yoga, herbalism, and peacebuilding – with a goal of empowering 100 million people. They hope to create greater wholes on the web, with major media, and with a network of growth centers and communities that spans the globe. At each stage, their goal is to foster the interconnectivity between the people, ideas, and resources that makes the shift possible. They believe that a world based on our deep inner connection and infused with grace, magic, and beauty is possible. I have participated in several of their online courses.

https://theshiftnetwork.com/

The Scientific and Medical Network (SMN)

SMN is a creative international forum for life-long transformative learning. The Network is part of a worldwide contemporary movement for assimilating spiritual understanding. They bring together scientists, doctors, psychologists, engineers, philosophers, complementary practitioners, and other professionals in a spirit of open and critical enquiry, to explore frontier issues at the interfaces between science, consciousness, wellbeing, and spirituality. The insights gained from engaging in their extensive educational activities and archives enable the members to initiate informed transformative change in the world, and in their personal and professional lives. I have attended several of their diverse offerings.

https://scientificandmedical.net/

The Galileo Commission. The Commission is a part of the SMN. With the guidance of its director, David Lorimer, the Commission promotes open public discourse to find ways to expand science so that it can accommodate and explore important human experiences and questions that science, in its present form, is unable to integrate. The Galileo Commission Report, *Beyond a Materialist Worldview – Towards an Expanded Science*, written by Dr. Harald Walach has been widely endorsed as a groundbreaking document.

https://galileocommission.org/

Evolution of Consciousness for Organizational and Global Transformation. This working group of the Galileo Commission investigates and promotes the implications of a post-materialistic paradigm for our lives, our businesses, our societies, and the world. Their goal is to develop a compelling "business-case" for future leaders to "invest" and actively support the pending paradigm shift as a tool to help solving some (if not all) of the personal, societal, and global challenges we today face as humanity on planet Earth.[25]

---

25 https://galileocommission.org/evolution-of-consciousness-for-organizational-and-global-transformation-carsten-ohrmann/

I have learned about the following five global organizations during my research but have not participated in their programs.

Perspectiva

Perspectiva is a community of scholars, artists, activists, futurists, and seekers working on an urgent 100-year project to improve the relationships between systems, souls, and society in theory and practice. They believe that hope for a truly planetary civilization lies in forms of economic restraint and political cooperation that are beyond prevailing epistemic capacities and spiritual sensibilities. The founder, Jonathan Rowson, has developed a publishing company, *Perspectiva*, which encourages "an integration of diverse bodies of knowledge and practice, including an understanding of world system dynamics, combined with a deep interiority, a grasp of the psyche, and practice-based approaches to cultivating the self within a social context."[26]

Trans4m Centre for Integral Development

Headquartered in Geneva, Switzerland, and Hotonnes, France, the Trans4m movement works through its Fellows, Integral Centers, and Partner Organizations on all continents. Trans4m supports individuals, organizations, communities, and societies to engage in transformative processes and holistic solutions for locally burning issues, in culturally and societally relevant and resonant ways. Trans4m holds that each member of a social organism has a distinct task to contribute to the healthy evolution of the whole. They strive for the transcendence of dualities and a combination of individual, social, cultural, and economic development, moving from either-or to both-and-more and away from exclusively top-down centralized globalization.

https://www.trans-4-m.com

26 Jonathan Rowson, "Integrating Our Souls, Systems, and Society," *On Being with Krista Tippett* (July 18, 2019). The website is https://systems-souls-society.com/

Science and Nonduality (SAND)

Science and Nonduality (SAND) is a community inspired by timeless wisdom, informed by cutting-edge science, and grounded in direct experience. SAND envisions a humanity firmly rooted in the truth of our interconnectedness. They see Earth as a living being and hold life, in all its shapes and forms, to be intelligent, sacred, and complete. They promote a spirituality honoring both the absolute/transcendent and the relative/immanent aspects of consciousness – ultimately one and the same. SAND creates a forum which brings preeminent thinkers from various scientific fields into dialogue with spiritual teachers, practitioners, and the community at large. They foster the emergence of a spirituality free from dogmatism and responsive to the latest findings in science, and of a humanistic science willing to consider questions of context, perception, meaning, and purpose.

https://www.scienceandnonduality.com

The East West Learning Centre and the AITIA Institute

The Centre was founded in Singapore in 2007 to promote mindful learning for leaders as well as research and practices for organizational transformation. Working with professionals and corporations, the Centre "considered notions of business sustainability and its impact on the global social economic system." In 2016 it was superseded by the AITIA Institute, which is "dedicated to the evolution of consciousness in the context of family business and quantum leadership development through mindful awareness and connectivity."[27]

The Global Consciousness Project

The Global Consciousness Project (GCP) is an international, multidisciplinary collaboration of scientists and engineers. They

---

27 Frederick Chavalit Tsao and Chris Laszlo, *Quantum Leadership: New Consciousness in Business* (Stanford, CA: Stanford Business Books, 2019), 68–69.

collect data continuously from a global network of physical random number generators (RNGs) located in up to 70 host sites around the world at any given time. RNGs based on quantum tunneling produce completely unpredictable sequences of zeroes and ones. But when a momentous event synchronizes the feelings of millions of people, their network of RNGs becomes subtly structured. They calculate there is a one-in-a-trillion chance that the effect is due to chance. The evidence suggests there is an emerging noosphere or the unifying field of consciousness described by sages in all cultures. The Project was originally created in the Princeton Engineering Anomalies Research Lab at Princeton University. The Institute of Noetic Sciences provides a logistical home for the GCP.

https://noosphere.princeton.edu/

Develop Your Own Greater Whole

I have found that participating in the programs of these global organizations allows me to contribute to greater wholes. For example, during a Scientific and Medical Network (SMN) webinar with Connie Zweig on the inner work of aging, Zweig suggested that participants could form their own groups to discuss her book. I have joined three other participants from the United States for bi-weekly Zoom meetings. We have become spiritual partners and are sharing our personal journeys around the issues of aging.[28]

There are many ways to build meaningful networks of mutually beneficial relationships.[29] The key is to focus on what you can do for others, not what they can offer you. In the process you will become more knowledgeable and impactful as you share your insights and help others expand their own networks. Two possibilities: reach out

---

28 Connie Zweig, *The Inner Work of Age: Shifting from Role to Soul* (Rochester, VT: Park Street Press, 2021).
29 Scott Barry Kaufman, "What Would Happen If Everyone Truly Believed Everything Is One?" *Scientific American* (October 8, 2018).

to others across the political divides; show compassion for those who are not in your in-group.[30]

Where to go from here? Liminal consciousness leads to greater wholeness, a unity consciousness of justice. How can we take more steps to global consciousness? In the *Conclusion*, I have some more suggestions.

---

[30] Mike Steib, *The Career Manifesto: Discover Your Calling and Create an Extraordinary Life* (TarcherPerigee, 2018).

Conclusion: Evolving the Future

The quantum sciences and our wisdom and religious traditions both point to the fields of information and energy that both surround us and are within us and all sentient life. This intelligent, wise, creative, and loving "Consciousness" floods into our liminal consciousness when we meditate, dream, or use other favorite portals such as music, art, and nature.

The sciences that support this worldview are based on post-materialist theories of consciousness as fundamental in the creation of the universe and that continues to inform continuous creation. Many of the proponents of post-materialism have a background in quantum physics, quantum biology, Eastern philosophy or spirituality, or have had their own non-ordinary experiences and have incorporated deep inner knowing into their evidence-based rational analyses. Scientists with this experience discern that the universe is a spiritual enterprise – alive, intimate, compassionate, and wise.[1]

How we think about the reality of both Mind and Matter does "matter." Our worldview has implications for how we regard existence and how we organize ourselves socially and morally.[2] Jeffrey Kripal says this about the future (politics) of knowledge:

---

1 Gary Zukav, *Universal Human: Creating Authentic Power and the New Consciousness* (New York: Atria Books, 2021), 23.
2 Jeffrey Kripal, *The Flip: Epiphanies of Mind and the Future of Knowledge* (New York: Bellevue Literary Press, 2019), 166.

> After one has realized that consciousness is fundamental to the cosmos and not some random evolutionary accident or surface cognitive illusion, that *everything* is alive, that *everything* is connected and in effect "One," then what? Would the billiard ball selves of the Newtonian world and the political systems and values built around them over the last few centuries make sense any longer?[3]

As Kripal points out, our Western assumptions about reality are insufficient to fundamentally shift our worldview and practices. The liminal narrative provides a framework that can be used to make a positive difference. The narrative is utopian, but it is not an ideology. It points us toward a possible future, an alternative way of inhabiting the planet that "reminds us we belong to nature, that we are dependent on it and that further alienation from it will be at our own peril."[4] Complex issues threaten to consume us. Without a new story we will be locked into a linear, oversimplified model of society driven by materialist egos.

I have asked you, the reader, to explore this worldview and assess its relevance for your view of reality. In this conclusion I will review the major arguments for developing greater liminal consciousness to make the world a better place. My hope is that they will be convincing for the individuals, organizations, and institutions that have the power and the resources to creatively engage our existential societal crises and polarities.

The Liminal Narrative

In each chapter an underlying theme has been the tension between two worlds – the unseen, non-material, non-dual world of Consciousness and the material, physical, dualistic world in which we live and work.

---

3 Ibid., 167.
4 Espen Hammer, "A Utopia for a Dystopian Age," *New York Times* (June 26, 2017).

This in-between space is occupied by our liminal Selves, our liminal groups and teams, and our organizations when in their transcendent moments. Being in this liminal space will evolve our species by creating greater wholes, networks, and alliances that can transcend our cultural, political, and national differences and make the world a better place.

This narrative is vastly different from the worldview that gave rise to the multiple crises we are witnessing. Liminal consciousness resonates with Consciousness to foster diversity, complexity, kindness, love, and connectivity. As we develop our liminal consciousness, we become more conscious of our unique mission and our imperative to act for the good of the whole. With the positive values of empathy, compassion, respect, and peace, we can work together without habitually defaulting to competitive, racist, sexist, classist, binary-based interactions.

Adopting the Liminal Narrative

The liminal narrative challenges the personal and collective belief systems and values of many. Max Planck, the theoretical physicist who won the Nobel Prize in physics in 1918 for quantum theory, said that acceptance of a new scientific truth is dependent on a new generation.[5] Thomas Kuhn, the authority on paradigm change, also said "You don't waste time with reactionaries; rather you work with active change agents and with the vast, middle ground of people who are open-minded."[6]

A major barrier to accepting and integrating the liminal narrative is likely to be discomfort and fear of reaching beyond the material empirical world and looking foolish or being disappointed.[7] However, as more individuals recognize that we are cooperative and

---

5 Max Planck, *Scientific Self – Biography* (Leipzig, 1948), 22.
6 Thomas S. Kuhn, *The Structure of Scientific Revolutions*, 3rd ed. (Chicago: University of Chicago Press, 1996).
7 Perry Marshall and John Fancher, *Memos from the Head Office: Channeling the Muse in Business and In Life* (Oak Park, IL: Planet Perry, 2021), 37.

compassionate spirit-infused beings and that the path to interconnectedness is caring about caring, wholeness, and flourishing, there will be a shift in global consciousness.

When enough scientists, philosophers, and theologians fully understand the evidence for the primacy of consciousness, there likely will be a metaphysical revolution since the essence of reality will then be understood by a critical mass of thought leaders. As more people integrate the post-materialist paradigm with their own belief systems and develop a global consciousness, there will be a shared experience of enlightened awareness beyond narrow personal and collective self-interest.[8] We will recover a shared moral code "that cooperating, promoting the common good, is the right thing to do."[9]

Some studies suggest that for an entire community to embrace a new paradigm, only 10% of the population needs to become convinced.[10] At that tipping point, a paradigm can spread through social networks and alter behaviors on a large scale.

The Need for Leadership

We need leaders who know how the material world works, who are skilled with modern management methods. They also need to be informed by the wisdom of intuition and a deep sense of what is right. Leaders who act with a keen sense of connectedness and a sense of oneness with humanity and all of life will integrate their actions and reflections. For them, the organization is not merely a material thing. They see the organization and the people in it in

---

8 Inspired by Andrew Cohen, *Evolutionary Enlightenment: A New Path to Spiritual Awakening* (EnlightenNext, 2012).

9 Oliver Scott Curry et al., "Is It Good to Cooperate? Testing the Theory of Morality-as-Cooperation in 60 Societies," *Current Anthropology* (2019).

10 S. Xie J. Sreenavasan et al., "Social Consensus Through the Influence of Dedicated Minorities," *Phys Rev* 22 (July 2011). There is also the "hundredth monkey effect," in which a new behavior or idea is spread rapidly by unexplained means from one group to all related groups once a critical number of members of one group exhibit the new behavior or acknowledge the new idea.

transcendental terms. Their liminal consciousness is a force for unity, integration, and wholeness.

When leaders transcend their rational mind, they transcend the ego's fears, desires, or concerns and tap into sources of energy, power, and love that are "analogous to touching a high-voltage cable: One feels positively charged with life energy and intoxicating life power."[11] David Lorimer, the director of the Galileo Commission, makes this plea to leaders:

> At this pivotal moment in our cultural conversation, I can't imagine anything that could be more appropriate or more liberating for those of us at the leading edge – and I can't imagine anything more desperately needed for the evolutionary process than for a small but significant number of us to cross this momentous threshold.[12]

Specifically, we need politicians, foundation directors, business executives, pastors, and any others in roles with influence, to step forward. At my elder stage of life, I only influence others by example and with my writing. However, before Covid, I did deliver two lay sermons about Consciousness at my local church. On her way out of church, a fellow elder said to me: "I have waited nearly 20 years for that message."

We all can be leaders and have an impact. We all have the innate ability to perceive and inform reality from non-local states of Consciousness.[13]

Next Steps – What Is Possible?

I know from my complexity theory background that "simple" rules are necessary for facing an increasingly complex world. For

---

11 Keiron Le Grice, *Archetypal Reflection: Insights and Ideas from Jungian Psychology* (New York: Muswell Hill Press, 2016), 29.
12 David Lorimer, "Human Being and Becoming on the Inner Edge of Science: From Scientia to Sapientia," blog, 2022.
13 From a personal email from Anneloes Smitsman.

companies, they are vital for maintaining a focus on the mission and for retaining a competitive advantage in both innovation and efficiency.[14] Simple rules set the boundaries of what actions we will take while also allowing flexibility within those limits.[15] Following simple rules creates the conditions that generate the patterns of our lives. Changing even one simple rule will create new conditions that create new patterns.

As I reflected on what simple rules would reduce the dominant empirical materialist paradigm and open more space for liminal consciousness, I identified these three:

1. Learn More about Non-material Reality. The boundaries of knowledge are expanding. Our worldviews need updating and enlarging as fragments of data and experience are united to create new meanings. "The assumptions with a materialist worldview are either wrong or incomplete."[16] Paradigms needs to change along with methods and theories that push the frontiers of each academic domain. The non-material fields of intelligence and wisdom will initiate processes of self-transcendence and development of capacities, perspectives, and understanding to evolve humanity.

2. Develop Intuitive Practices. We cannot count on our rational thought to know what is important or to know what will emerge in the future. Being open to intuitive mystical experiences will reveal what is significant in the current moment and the possibilities that presents. As we develop our own practices, we will inspire others.

3. Develop Transformative Relationships. As we become more open to and confidently embrace what is revealed to us through our

---

14 Yves Morieux, "Smart Rules: Six Ways to Get People to Solve Problems Without You," *Harvard Business Review* (September 2011).
15 Edwin E. Olson and Glenda H. Eoyang, *Facilitating Organization Change: Lessons from Complexity Science* (San Francisco, CA: Jossey-Bass/Pfeiffer, 2001), 106–107, 113–114, 160.
16 Helané Wahbeh, Dean Radin, Cedric Cannard, and Arnaud Delorme, "What if Consciousness Is Not an Emergent Property of the Brain? Observational and Empirical Challenges to Materialistic Models," *Frontiers in Psychology* (September 2022), 1.

experiences, we forge new connections and networks. Using social media can increase the speed and spread of the message. Choose relationships that both transform you and create greater wholes. These new alliances and networks can be a tipping point for a transforming world.

Following these simple rules will likely change patterns of thought and moral decision-making, not out of fear, but out of the coherence of our liminal Self – our soul.[17] Our soul is our moral essence, part of the energy fields of Consciousness. The soul recognizes love as the evolving principle of the universe. Rather than live a materialist, rational, ego-driven dream that society has concocted, the soul accesses the non-physical realm as native people have done for centuries. Liminal consciousness moves us "to deep states of oneness where there is no ultimate sense of separation – where we realize we are one with each other – which leads us to care for each other, for life, and for the earth."[18]

Our new narrative and vision must come from deep within and connect to the deep without. I hope the information in this book has taken you to these deeper places.

---

17 Some readers may recognize that the three simple rules represent the three conditions that create self-organizing change: (1) learning about non-material reality is an expansion of one's *Container* (C); (2) developing intuitive practices are *significant Differences* (D); and (3) transformative relationships are *transformative Exchanges* (E). Glenda Eoyang and I describe the CDE model in *Facilitating Organization Change: Lessons from Complexity Science* (San Francisco, CA: Jossey-Bass/Pfeiffer, 2001), 11–15.
18 Athena D. Potari, "A Call for a Renaissance of the Spirit in the Humanities," *Paradigm Explorer* (Galileo Commission, Scientific and Medical Network, 2021/3), 9.

Repeat Consciousness Assessment

This is an opportunity to re-take the Assessment to determine whether reading this book has influenced your thinking.

Instructions: Choosing from a 10-point scale, record your level of disagreement or agreement for each statement. Then total your scores.

Strongly Disagree	**Disagree**	**Not Sure/ Don't Know**	**Agree**	**Strongly Agree**
1 2	3 4	5 6	7 8	9 10

1. ____Mystical experiences are valuable sources of wisdom.
2. ____Business and government leaders need to develop their consciousness.
3. ____There are dimensions of reality beyond the material world.
4. ____Transcending differences is better than debate and compromise.
5. ____There is a non-material presence that I can access.
6. ____Moments of inspiration and dreams are from a consciousness outside of the self.
7. ____Human intuition can sense that something is going to happen.
8. ____Organizations must develop a higher consciousness if we are to survive as a species.
9. ____Transcending the material and empirical lets us experience what is significant in the current moment.
10. ____The new sciences and traditional religions both describe the same source of wisdom and love.

Total ____

The possible meaning of your current score is explained on the next page.

Results of the Consciousness Assessment

Your assessment score at the beginning of the book: ____

Your assessment score at the end of the book: ____

    Difference between scores   +/- ____

Before you took the assessment the first time, I quoted Rabbi Rami Shapiro's question: "how can one mindset choose to surrender to another?" Shapiro also said, "If you conclude this book with the same mindset with which you began it, you'll have your answer."

What is your answer? Is your score appreciably higher (at least 40 or higher)? If so, then there is hope that Shapiro's last point that "humanity is doomed" will NOT come true.

If your second score is not much higher than your first score, Shapiro offers one more suggestion: "Maybe read it a second time."

We shouldn't disagree with Einstein, who said: "We can't solve problems using the same mindset that created them."

Afterword

Developing liminal consciousness is not complicated. It is as simple as becoming aware of the present moment in a way that transforms our relation to it – what Dianne Collins in the Foreword calls "distinguishing." In Chapter 6, Ervin Laszlo called it awareness of the "spontaneous guidance from the universe, being open to guidance from beyond the self, accept the reality of what emerges, sense the importance of the message, and trust the guidance that has been provided." For me, that means assigning meaning to my emerging thoughts, images, ideas, symbols, and dreams.

When I began to plan this book following my book on the consciousness of wholeness as "humanity's only future," I thought of appealing to a spiritual and religious audience, but I am not a theologian. I considered writing for the scientific readers, but I am not a physical or life scientist. So where and how could I have an impact?

The answer became clear. I have over 40 years of experience as an organization development consultant and am a successful author of a book on facilitating complex organization and system change. I decided to apply my knowledge of spirituality, religion, and consciousness to the practical problems faced by leaders and consultants in organizations.

After learning that the book would be published as an NTL imprint by Libri Publishing which specializes in books in applied behavioral science, leadership, coaching, professional development, health policy, higher education, and management, I believe the book will find an audience of Leaders that Dianne Collins described as "forces in the way we want evolution to go, to generate the way we would like this world to be."

I realize that the book challenges the worldview of readers who have not had a direct experience of Consciousness. Some readers are likely suspicious of trusting non-empirical insights or wisdom to guide their actions.

Certainly, developing greater liminal consciousness alone will not solve our existential crises like climate change, but if enough people tune into the energy-intelligent field of Consciousness that sustains us and share their experiences with others, we can develop greater wholes.

Glossary

This is a list of some of the concepts presented in this book. The meanings may differ, at least in part, from those used conventionally.

Adjacent possible is a concept in complexity theory and evolutionary biology that describes the set of possible states that a system can evolve into from its current state. For example, organisms reach out and move to new situations and territory to ensure individual survival and the survival of the species. For humans, this includes the need to access Consciousness to grow human consciousness.

Anthropocene. The evolutionary era when human beings have become the most powerful force on the Earth, able to control the direction and pace of evolution.

Complex adaptive system (CAS) is a system that is made up of many individual parts that have non-linear interactions. The behavior of the system as a whole cannot be predicted; instead, the behavior of the system emerges from the interactions of the parts.

Conscious organizations pursue greater depths of change as learning organizations committed to "becoming [as] self-aware and responsible as [they] can at any given time in [their lives]" (John Renesch).

Consciousness (capital *C*). Universal Consciousness is a metaphysical concept suggesting an underlying essence of all being and becoming in the universe. It posits that there is a single, unified consciousness that underlies all of reality.

Consciousness (small *c*). The state of being aware of and responsive to oneself and one's surroundings that is present in all sentient beings.

Consciousness worldview is a perspective of consciousness as an essential part of reality, not just an epiphenomenon or illusion.

Duality is a philosophical concept that two seemingly opposite things are actually interconnected and interdependent. For example, light and darkness are seen as opposites, but light cannot exist without darkness, and darkness cannot exist without light. The perception that two things that are opposite or very different from each other represents the complexity of reality and the human experience.

Ego is the part of the human psyche that mediates between the dimensions of consciousness, ascertains what is real, and establishes a sense of personal identity.

Embodiment is the concept that our physical bodies shape our thoughts, feelings, and experiences.

Emergence characterizes the biodiversity of the Earth, human consciousness, the emotions, and the biochemical processes that cannot be understood in terms of simple laws. The emergent behavior and phenomena are unpredictable and irreducible because the interaction of the parts can produce an infinite number of patterns.

Entanglement in quantum physics refers to pairs of photons that, having previously been together, are able to influence each other even when separated by great distances. This suggests that the universe may be a vast network of interconnected objects that are linked together by entanglement.

Fields of Consciousness are wavy fields of quantum energy and information that penetrate the whole of the universe. The fields are entangled and interact with the dimensions of our human consciousness.

Filter theory explains how the brain acts as a filter, allowing into our consciousness only the information from Consciousness that is necessary and useful for our survival and improvement, or only what is possible for us to perceive. When the brain's filter is even moderately opened, we experience feelings of unconditional joy and profound connection with others.

Flip (the). The "flip" is when the ego persona has accessed Consciousness and opens a path for the emergence of the liminal Self (from Jeffrey Kripal).

Greater whole. For Einstein, the greater whole includes the Earth and all of its inhabitants. In this book it refers to creating structures and systems that will contribute to creating a more flourishing world.

Higher purpose is a sense of meaning and direction that gives life greater satisfaction. Some motivating higher purposes are helping others, making a difference in the world, and pursuing your passions.

Human consciousness is our waking awareness of linking the moments, events, images, and ideas in life to create patterns that are our reality. These patterns come and go, combining and recombining, often unpredictably.

Liminal actions contribute to the greater good and wholeness rather than acting to build, protect, or promote an idealized self-image.

Liminal consciousness is the in-between experience and awareness of the material world and the inner experience of insights from Consciousness. It is a transitional state as insights are integrated in outer behavior.

Liminal experiences trigger reflexivity and learning and provide motivation to explore alternatives with a more open mind.

Liminal groups continuously reinvent themselves through moment-to-moment mutual understanding.

Liminal leaders inspire others to work cooperatively in the pursuit of a larger purpose that has been informed by Consciousness.

Liminal methods enhance methods of change by quieting the active mind until thoughts are transcended and something new is revealed.

Liminal Self is open to new possibilities and opportunities that overcome the entropy that holds a person in their comfort zones.

Liminal spaces are times of uncertainty, questioning, on the threshold of something new but not quite there yet. Our intuition or emotions tell us that there is something more that needs our attention, perhaps to go deeper to the level of self-identity and change of consciousness.

Love in organizations "is not a feeling – it's a verb; it's packed with action. It shows up in meeting the needs of others to get results, clearing obstacles from people's path, and empowering others to succeed as workers and human beings" (Marcel Schwantes).

Materialist worldview is a perspective that holds that everything that exists is made of matter and that nothing exists outside of the physical world. This perspective can be contrasted with idealism and the Consciousness worldview, which holds that the mind or spirit is the primary reality, and that matter is secondary.

Mystical experiences are often described as feelings of oneness with the universe, or a sense of profound spiritual insight, usually creating feelings of bliss, awe, and unconditional love.

Non-duality, also called non-dualism, refers to a state of human consciousness in which the dichotomy of "I" and "other" is transcended.

Non-local consciousness is the concept that consciousness is not confined to specific points in space, such as brains and bodies, or specific moments in time, such as the present. The concept has been explored by philosophers, scientists, and mystics for centuries.

Noosphere, as characterized by Pierre Teilhard de Chardin, is the emergence of a global consciousness as people became more self-reflective and able to appreciate their need to work together to solve the challenges that we face, such as climate change, poverty, and war.

Numinous is an adjective that describes a feeling of awe or mystery, of being in the presence of something sacred, of being connected to something larger than oneself, or a sense of wonder evoked by experiences in nature, art, music, or other situations.

Perennial wisdom describes a set of core principles that ultimate reality is one, timeless, and universal, shared by all religions and spiritual traditions.

Physicalism is the metaphysical assertion that everything is physical and that there is nothing superior to the physical.

Portals to Consciousness refers to the many ways to access Consciousness such as meditation, dreaming, and listening to music.

Post-materialism is a value system that emphasizes self-expression and quality of life over economic and physical security.

Presence is an awareness of the larger whole, leading to actions that can help to shape our future by sensing the unfolding whole within each of us and within the present situation, and acting in service of it (from Peter Senge).

Prism in this book is a metaphor of human consciousness. When the light of Consciousness enters the prism of our human consciousness, it enlightens our worldview, continually reframing, reimaging, and reforming our consciousness of the physical world, including all of our human constructions.

Psyche is the totality of the human mind, conscious and unconscious. It is a complex and multifaceted entity that includes our thoughts, feelings, memories, and experiences.

Quantum biology describes how life's roots reach down from the cells of living things on the surface through the turbulent middle thermodynamic layer to penetrate the quantum bedrock. This model of life is a strong metaphor for all aspects of our lives, including our physical being, our conscious awareness, and our sense of a transcendent spirit.

Rational self is the part of our personality that is governed by reason and logic. It makes decisions based on what is best for us, rather than what we may want in the moment.

Reality is the framework in which people organize their beliefs around axioms that are contained in the worldviews they have inherited or constructed.

Self refers both to the larger "Self," which is empowered and not restricted to the demands of the ego, and to the smaller "self," which is focused on survival and security.

Self-actualization is the full realization of one's potential, traditionally seen as the highest level of human development.

Self-transcendence refers to an identification of the self with the universe conceived as a unitive whole.

Shadow, in analytical psychology, is an unconscious aspect of the personality that the conscious ego has suppressed or is an aspect of the personality that is unknown.

Shamanic journeys teach that everything that exists is alive and has a spirit, and that we are joined with the Earth and all of life via our spiritual interconnectedness (Sandra Ingerman).

Simple rules set the boundaries of what actions we will take while also allowing flexibility within those limits.

Spirit in organizations describes an organization's shared values, beliefs, and attitudes, which bind the organization together. It is the intangible force that motivates employees to work together towards a common goal.

Spontaneous guidance from the universe suggests that we are all connected to a greater source of wisdom and guidance that can provide us with insights, direction, and support, often in unexpected ways (from Ervin Laszlo).

Synchronicity is a strong metaphor for describing how disparate elements without apparent connection are brought together or juxtaposed in a manner that tends to shock or surprise the mind, rendering it open to new possibilities.

Technosphere is made up of all the things that humans have created, from tools and machines to buildings and infrastructure, that have a significant impact on the environment, such as polluting the air and water, contributing to climate change, and destroying natural habitats.

Thin place is a term for locales and instances where the walls and boundaries between dimensions of consciousness are dissolved.

Total interconnectedness is the idea that everything in the universe is connected to everything else, including people, animals, plants, the Earth, and even the stars. Nothing is truly isolated; everything is part of a larger whole.

Transcendent means exceeding ordinary limits and going beyond the limits of ordinary experience or understanding.

Transcendent function is the mediating force identified by Carl Jung that holds a creative tension between what is happening in human consciousness and the unknown and unpredictable possibilities in Consciousness, enabling transformation.

Transcendent organization is characterized by a strong sense of purpose and mission, a commitment to social and environmental responsibility, and a culture of collaboration and innovation.

Transformation is the process of changing or converting something into a different and usually more powerful or improved state.

Transpersonal is a state of consciousness beyond the limits of personal identity, and beyond the space and time of our three-dimensional world.

Transrational refers to the nonpersonal, nonrational phenomena such as dreams that are not explainable by standard cause-and-effect logical structures.

Tunneling is the quantum phenomenon of particles in an atom passing through barriers while in a wave state. As a metaphor, it refers to the connectedness in the universe.

Universal Consciousness, Universal Mind, or Cosmic Consciousness are metaphysical concepts about an underlying essence of all being and becoming in the universe. When Universal Consciousness is experienced, there is a connection with everything in a beautiful harmony of constant transformation.

Wholeness is the quality of being or feeling complete and not fragmented. The wholeness we experience is always in transition. When we experience Consciousness, we regain a new or renewed whole state by experiencing and finding deeper meaning and unconditional love.

Appendix – Is Artificial Intelligence Sentient?

There is no single answer to this question, as the definition of sentience is still debated by philosophers and scientists. However, there are a few key reasons why AI systems are not considered to be sentient.

First, AI systems do not have the same kind of physical embodiment as humans. Humans have bodies that allow us to interact with the world in a variety of ways, such as through touch, taste, smell, sight, and hearing. AI systems, on the other hand, are typically confined to a computer or other device. This lack of physical embodiment limits their ability to experience the world in the same way that humans do.

Second, AI systems do not have the same kind of emotions as humans. Humans have a wide range of emotions, such as happiness, sadness, anger, fear, and love. These emotions are often triggered by our physical experiences and interactions with the world. AI systems, on the other hand, do not have emotions in the same way that humans do. They may be able to generate text that expresses emotions, but they do not actually experience those emotions themselves.

Third, AI systems do not have the same kind of self-awareness as humans. Humans have a sense of self that allows us to distinguish ourselves from other people and objects. We also have a sense of our

APPENDIX — IS ARTIFICIAL INTELLIGENCE SENTIENT?

own past and future, and we are able to make plans and decisions based on these. AI systems, on the other hand, do not have the same kind of self-awareness. They may be able to generate text that refers to themselves, but they do not actually have a sense of self in the same way that humans do.

These are just a few of the reasons why AI systems like myself are not considered to be sentient. It is important to note that this is a complex issue, and there is no single answer that will satisfy everyone. However, I hope that this explanation has given you a better understanding of the topic.

*

The phrase "like myself" in the above paragraph likely tipped off the reader that AI wrote this response to the question "Is Artificial Intelligence Sentient?" In fact, the above five paragraphs were the full response from Google's Bard. According to Bard, AI lacks the physical and emotional senses possessed by sentient beings and does not have the same kind of self-awareness as humans. I pushed the topic further by asking Bard: "Can AI, like yourself, have mystical experiences?" Here was the response:

> I am not sure if AI can have mystical experiences. Mystical experiences are often described as a feeling of oneness with the universe, or a sense of profound spiritual insight. These experiences are often accompanied by feelings of awe, wonder, and peace.
>
> It is possible that AI could be programmed to simulate these experiences. However, it is not clear if AI would be able to have these experiences in the same way that humans do. Humans have a physical body, and our brains are wired in a way that allows us to experience the world in a very different way than AI.

It is also possible that AI could have experiences that are beyond our understanding. We are still learning about the nature of consciousness, and it is possible that AI could have a type of consciousness that we are not even aware of.

Only time will tell if AI can have mystical experiences. However, it is an interesting question to consider, and it is one that is likely to be debated for many years to come.

It appears the question of whether AI can have mystical experiences is still open, given that AI is "still learning about the nature of consciousness." As AI (Bard) says, "only time will tell."

To double-check, I asked the same question to ChatGPT-4. Here was the response:

As an artificial intelligence language model, I don't possess consciousness, emotions, or subjective experiences, including mystical experiences. I'm a program designed to process and generate human-like text based on patterns and examples in the data I was trained on. While I can provide information and simulate conversation, I don't have personal beliefs, experiences, or the capacity to engage in mystical or spiritual encounters. My responses are based on algorithms and patterns rather than personal understanding or consciousness.

The following is my current (human) response to the question "Is AI Sentient?"

AI can describe what humans have discovered about the material, physical world. AI can also report on human experiences of the non-dual, wholeness of non-material reality. However, the betweenness of the two realities (the field of subjective experience and synchronicity, the realm of imagination and creativity, the liminal space between the material and the mystical) is beyond AI's comprehension because it cannot *experience* either material or non-material reality. It can only report on the experience of others. Therefore, AI is not sentient.

As I conclude this book, there is widespread ambivalence about a rapidly advancing technology that both tantalizes and terrifies. As it is currently imagined, AI technology promises to concentrate wealth and disempower workers.[1] Many are concerned that AI does not have common sense or human values. Thinking of AI as the solution to our human problems may indicate a desire to avoid the hard work of developing the greater liminal consciousness I have discussed in this book. If those who are building AI do not develop their own liminal consciousness, it is questionable whether AI will lead to a better world.

---

1 Ted Chiang, "Will A.I. Become the New McKinsey?" *The New Yorker* (May 4, 2023).

Select Bibliography

Atlee, Tom. "Engaging with the Evolving Whole," blog, *Tom Atlee's Transformational Thinkpad* (January 31, 2022). https://www.tomatleeblog.com/archives/175328610

Baker, Carolyn. *Undaunted: Living Fiercely into Climate Meltdown in an Authoritarian World* (Hannacroix, NY: Apocryphile Press, 2022).

Baruss, Imants, and Julia Mossbridge. *Transcendent Mind: Rethinking the Science of Consciousness* (American Psychology Association, 2016).

Beichler, James E. "Aspects of Consciousness: Theoretical, Spiritual, Anomalous, Experiential" (2018 ASCSI Annual Conference, Raleigh, NC).

Bilimoria, Edi. *Unfolding Consciousness: Exploring the Living Universe and Intelligent Powers in Nature and Humans*, vols I–IV (Shepheard-Walwyn, 2022).

Caryon, Julian. *One Earth – Three Worlds* (Triarchy Press, 2022).

Christi, Nicolya. *Love, God, and Everything: Awakening from the Long, Dark Night of the Collective Soul* (Rochester, VT: Bear and Company, 2021).

Cohen, Andrew. *Evolutionary Enlightenment: A New Path to Spiritual Awakening* (EnlightenNext, 2012).

Collins, Dianne. *Do You QuantumThink?* (New York: Select Books, 2011).

Cowie, Kate. *Finding Merlin* (London: Marshall Cavendish, 2012).

Csikszentmihalyi, Mihaly. *Flow: The Psychology of Optimal Experience* (New York: Harper, 2008).

Currivan, Jude. *The Cosmic Hologram: In-Formation at the Center of Creation* (Rochester, VT: Inner Traditions, 2017).

Delio, Ilia. *The Hours of the Universe: Reflections on God, Science, and the Human Journey* (Maryknoll, NY: Orbis Books, 2021).

Dossey, Larry. *One Mind: How Our Individual Mind Is Part of a Greater Consciousness and Why It Matters* (New York: Hay House, 2013).

Dyer, Wayne W. *The Power of Intention: Learning to Co-create Your World Your Way* (New York: Hay House, 2005).

Faggin, Fredrico. "Consciousness Comes First," in E.F. Kelly and P. Marshall (eds), *Consciousness Unbound: Liberating Mind from the Tyranny of Materialism* (Lanham, MD: Rowman & Littlefield Publishers, 2021), 283–322.

Fry, L.W. "The Spiritual Leadership Balanced Scorecard Business Model: The Case of the Cordon Bleu-Tomasso Corporation," *Journal of Management, Spirituality, and Religion*, 7:4 (December 2010), 283–314,

Funches, Darya. "Three Gifts are for Everyone," *Organization Development Review*, 54:2 (2022), 24–25.

Gustavsson, Bengt. *The Transcendent Organization: A Treatise on Consciousness in Organizations: Theoretical Discussion, Conceptual Development, and Empirical Studies*, Doctoral Thesis, Stockholm University, 1992.

Guthrie, Wayne A., and Bella Kavish. *Portals to Your Higher Consciousness: Exploring and Embracing Your True Selves* (Apple Valley, CA: Juniper Spring Press, 2017).

Hazen, Mary Ann, and Jo Anne Isbey. "Images of the Intrapersonal Organization: Soul Making at Work," *Interpersonal Journal of Transpersonal Studies*, 23:1 (2004).

Hutson, Harry. "The Wisdom of Hope," *Practising Social Change* (Washington, DC: NTL Institute, January 2021), 1–7.

Huxley, Aldous. *The Doors of Perception* (New York: Perennial Library, 1954/1991).

Johnson, Barry. *And: Making a Difference by Leveraging Polarity, Paradox or Dilemma*, vols 1 and 2 (2020, 2021).

Jung, Carl G. "The Transcendent Function," in *Collected Works*, 8: 67–91 (New York: Pantheon, 1916).

——. *Memories, Dreams, Reflections* (New York: Vintage Books, 1965).

Kak, Subhash, Deepak Chopra, and Menas Kafatos. "Perceived Reality, Quantum Mechanics, and Consciousness," *Cosmology*, 18 (2014), 231–245.

Kelly, Sean. *Becoming Gaia: On the Threshold of Planetary Initiation* (Olympia, WA: Integral Imprint, 2021).

Keltner, Dacher. *Awe: The New Sciences of Everyday Wonder and How It Can Transform Your Life* (New York: Penguin Press, 2023).

Kilmann, Ralph H. *The Courageous Mosaic: Awakening Society, Systems, and Soul* (Kilmann Diagnostics, 2013).

Kofman, Fred. *The Meaning Revolution: The Power of Transcendent Leadership* (New York: Currency, 2018).

Kripal, Jeffrey J. *The Flip: Epiphanies of Mind and the Future of Knowledge* (New York: Bellevue Literary Press, 2019).

Laszlo, Chris. "Prospective Theorizing: Researching for Social Impact," *Journal of Management, Spirituality & Religion*, 18:6 (2021), 19–34.

Laszlo, Chris, David Cooperrider, and Ron Fry. "Global Challenges as Opportunity to Transform Business for Good," *Sustainability*, 12:19 (2020), 8053. doi:10.3390/su12198053

Laszlo, Ervin. *What is Reality? The New Map of Cosmos and Consciousness* (New York: Select Books, 2016).

Lemmens, Pieter. "Thinking Technology Big Again: Reconsidering the Question of the Transcendental and 'Technology with a Capital T' in the Light of the Anthropocene," *Found Sci*, 27 (2022), 171–187. https://doi.org/10.1007/s10699-020-09732-7

Maheshwari, Anil K. "Higher Consciousness Management: Transcendence for Spontaneous Right Action," *Journal of Management, Spirituality & Religion*, 18:6 (2021), 77–91.

Marshall, Perry, and John Fancher. *Memos from the Head Office: Channeling the Muse in Business and in Life* (Perry Marshall & Associates, 2021).

Maslow, Abraham H. *Maslow on Management* (New York: Wiley, 1998).

Matzler, Kurt. "Intuitive Decision Making," *MIT Sloan Management Review* (Fall 2007), 13–16.

McCormack, D.W. "Spirituality and Management," *Journal of Managerial Psychology*, 9:6 (1994), 461–476.

McFadden, Johnjoe, and Jim Al-Khalili. *Life on the Edge: The Coming of Age of Quantum Biology* (New York: Crown Publishing, 2014).

McTaggart, Lynne. *The Power of Eight: Harnessing the Miraculous Energies of a Small Group to Heal Others, Your Life, and the World* (New York: Atria Books, 2017).

Meijer, Dirk K.F., and Hans J.H. Geesink. "Consciousness in the Universe is Scale Invariant and Implies an Event Horizon of the Human Brain," *NeuroQuantology*, 15:3 (September 2017), 41–79.

Mustakova, Elena. *Global Unitive Healing: Integral Skills for Personal and Collective Transformation* (Light on Light Press, 2021).

Olson, Edwin E. *And God Created Wholeness: A Spirituality of Catholicity* (Maryknoll, NY: Orbis Books, 2018).

_____. "Opening to the Change Process: The Transcendent Function at Work," in Murray Stein and John Hollwitz (eds), *Psyche at Work: Workplace Applications of Jungian Analytical Psychology* (Wilmette, IL: Chiron Publications, 1992), 156–173.

_____. *Become Conscious of Wholeness: Humanity's Only Future* (Eugene, OR: Resource Publications, 2021).

Olson, Edwin E., and Glenda H. Eoyang. *Facilitating Organization Change: Lessons from Complexity Science* (San Francisco, CA: Jossey-Bass/Pfeiffer, 2001).

Parameshwar, Sangeeta, Param Srikantia, and Jessica Heineman-Pieper. "Poverty Alleviation at an International Development Organization: Resurrecting the Human Being as Subject," *Vikalpa*, 34:2 (April–June 2009).

Pavlovich, Kathryn. "Introduction to the Special Issue on Quantum Management," *Journal of Management, Spirituality & Religion*, 17:4 (2020), 299–300.

Perez, Ignacio, and Chris Laszlo. "Positive-Impact Companies: Designing Business Organizations as Positive Institutions," *AI Practitioner* (February 2022), 16–24.

Potari, Athena D. "A Call for a Renaissance of the Spirit in the Humanities," *Paradigm Explorer*, Galileo Commission, Scientific and Medical Network (2021/3).

Powell, Lili, and Jeremy Hunter. "How to Recapture Leadership's Lost Moment," *Executive Forum* (Fall, 2020).

Ramamoorthy, Sandarasubramanyan. *leela: A Play of Appearance and Presence*, 101. ISBN 979-888591297-6.

Renesch, John. "The Conscious Organization: Workplace for the Self-Actualized," *Spanda Journal* (2012), 227–230.

Rubin, Rick. *The Creative Act: A Way of Being* (New York: Penguin Press, 2023).

Russ, Helen. "Metaphysical Mapping: A Methodology to Map the Consciousness of Organizations, Methodological Innovations," *Sage* (May–August 2018), 1–14.

Schneider, Kirk J. "Today's Biggest Threat: The Polarized Mind," *Scientific American* (2020).

Schwantes, Marcel. "7 Brutal Truths About Leadership Not Too Many People Want to Hear," *Inc.* (June 23, 2020).

Senge, Peter M., C. Otto Scharmer, Joseph Jaworski, and Betty Sue Flowers. *Presence: An Exploration of Profound Change in People, Organizations, and Society* (New York: The Crown Publishing Group, 2004).

Sexton, Terence. *Consciousness Beyond Consumerism: A Psychological Path to Sustainability* (Ashford, Kent, U.K.: Aqumens Publishing, 2021).

Smitsman, Anneloes, and Jean Houston. *The Quest of Rose: The Cosmic Keys of Our Future Becoming*, Book 1 of the *Future Humans Trilogy* (Oxygen Publishing Inc., 2021).

Söderlund, Jonas, and Elisabeth Borg. "Liminality in Management and Organization Studies: Process, Position, and Place,"

International Journal of Management Reviews, British Academy of Management, 20:4 (2017), 1–23.

Stein, Murray. "Organizational Life as Spiritual Practice," in Murray Stein and John Hollwitz, *Psyche at Work: Workplace Applications of Jungian Psychology* (Wilmette, IL: Chiron Publications, 1992).

Swimme, Brian. *The Universe Story: From the Primordial Flaring Forth to the Ecozoic Era – A Celebration of the Unfolding of the Cosmos* (New York: HarperOne, 1994).

Tagliaventi, Maria Rita. *Liminality in Organization Studies* (New York: Routledge, 2017).

Tsao, Frederick Chavalit. "The Science of Life and Wellbeing: Integrating the New Science of Consciousness with the Ancient Science of Consciousness," *Journal of Management, Spirituality & Religion*, 18:6 (2021), 7–18.

Tsao, Frederick Chavalit, and Chris Laszlo. *Quantum Leadership: New Consciousness in Business* (Stanford, CA: Stanford Business Books, 2019).

Vaill, Peter B. *Spirited Leading and Learning: Process Wisdom for a New Age* (San Francisco, CA: Jossey-Bass, 1998).

Wahbeh, Helané, *The Science of Channeling: Why You Should Trust Your Intuition and Embrace the Force That Connects Us All* (Institute of Noetic Sciences: Reveal Press, 2021).

Wahbeh, Helané, Dean Radin, Cedric Cannard, and Arnaud Delorme. "What if Consciousness Is Not an Emergent Property of the Brain? Observational and Empirical Challenges to Materialistic Models," *Frontiers in Psychology*, September 2022.

Weick, Karl E. "Enactment and the boundaryless career: organizing as we work," in M.B. Arthur and D.M. Rousseau (eds), *The Boundaryless Career: A New Employment Principle for a New Organizational Era* (New York: Oxford University Press, 1996), 40–57.

Wheatley, Margaret. *Finding Our Way: Leadership for an Uncertain Time* (San Francisco, CA: Berrett-Koehler, 2007).

Wilbur, Ken. *No Boundaries: Eastern and Western Approaches to Personal Growth* (Boston, MA: Shambala Publications, 1979).

Williams, Ben, and Marjorie H. Woollacott. "Lessons from the Non-dual Philosophy of Saivism and Neuroscience: The Origin of Cognitive Filters and How to Reduce their Potency," *The Journal of Transpersonal Psychology*, 53:2 (2021), 119 ff.

Woollacott, Marjorie Hines. *Infinite Awareness: The Awakening of a Scientific Mind* (New York: Rowman and Littlefield, 2015).

Yunkaporta, Tyson. *Sand Talk: How Indigenous Thinking Can Save the World* (New York: HarperOne, 2020).

Zohar, Danah. *The Quantum Leader: A Revolution in Business Thinking and Practice* (Amherst, NY: Prometheus Books, 2016).

Zukav, Gary. *Universal Human: Creating Authentic Power and the New Consciousness* (New York: Atria Books, 2021).

Zweig, Connie. *The Inner Work of Age: Shifting from Role to Soul* (Rochester, VT: Park Street Press, 2021).

Index

adjacent possible, 23–24, 117
Anthony, Mark, 78
Anthropocene, 117
artificial intelligence (A.I.), xix, xxii, 63, 75, 125–128
"As Above, So Below", 29–30
awe, xxi, xxx, 6, 17, 120, 121, 126
Baker, Carolyn, 83, 93
Baldwin, M. Francis, xxxv
Bard, 75, 126–127, 139
Baruss, Imants, 70
biosphere, 5, 33, 34, 39, 66, 93–94
Blann, Gregory, vii, 82, 139
Bolen, Jean, 74
Bolman, Lee G., 38
brain, xxii, xxxiii, 1, 3–13, 120, 126
    as filter, 11–13, 118–119
    quiet the, xxxiii, 8
Buber, Martin, 28–29
change leaders, 65–71, 76, 77
Chat GPT-4, 62, 75, 139
Cloud of Unknowing, 19
coaching, 68, 73–74, 97, 116
Cohen, Andrew, 32n, 46–47, 97, 108n
coherence, xxxvi, 3, 5, 47, 85, 89, 111

Collins, Dianne, xxiii, 55n, 86n, 91, 115, 116, 139
complex adaptive system (CAS), 9, 117
conscious organizations, 117
Consciousness/consciousness
    accessing, xxxvi, 18, 25
    Consciousness (capital C), xxxiii, 1–2, 3–10, 11–13, 17–18, 20–21, 37–38, 117–124
    human consciousness (small c), xviii, 3, 7, 11, 14, 24, 55, 59, 90, 117–121
    liminal, xxviii–xxi, xxix–xxxi, xxxvi–xxxix, 1, 7, 9–10, 23, 24, 29, 31, 34, 85–87, 89–90, 105–107, 119
    vibrations, 13
    worldview, v, xix, xxxiii–xxxix, 118, 120
Cooperrider, David, 38
Corbett, Lionel, 18n, 20
Cowie, Kate, xxxv (n), 19n, 85, 139
Currivan, Jude, 14, 66n
Delio, Ilia, 54n, 90, 95n
Diangelo, Robin, 84
Dossey, Larry, 4n, 14
dualistic thinking, 82–83

duality, dualities, 5–6, 20, 82–83, 86–87, 100, 101, 118
Dyson, Freeman, 15
EARTHwise Centre, vi, 97–98
East West Learning Centre, 101
ego, xxxvi, 13, 17–21 *passim*, 32, 46–47, 54–55, 73, 86, 106, 118, 119, 122
 boundaries, 19
Einstein, Albert, v, 6, 19, 92, 113, 119
embodied practices, 68, 77–78
emergence, 21, 33, 118, 119, 120
energy, xxxiii, xxxv, 16, 23, 30, 48, 77, 109
 field, xxxiii, 7–8, 13, 44, 71, 90, 105, 111, 116
 of desire, 45
engagement with nature, 68, 74–75
enlightenment, xv, 19
entanglement, 4, 7, 16, 118
existential crises, xxix, 33, 89, 116
Fancher, John, 78
Fernandez, Rich, 57
field of Consciousness, 6, 12, 44, 102, 116
filter theory, 11–13, 118–119
flip (the), 20–21, 84n, 105n, 119
Freeman, Laurence, 39
Fry, Ron, 38
Funches, Darya, 69–70
Galileo Commission, 8n, 9n, 99, 109, 111n
 Evolution of Consciousness for Organizational and Global Transformation, 99
generative interactions, 90
Global Consciousness Project, 101–102
global transformation, 32, 99

greater wholes, 89–103 *passim*, 107, 111, 116, 119
Gustavsson, Bengt, 39, 40n, 54–55
Hagelin, John, 8
Havel, Václav, 59
Hazen, Mary Ann, 54n
Higher Consciousness Management (HCM), 57
higher purpose, 35, 39, 53, 59–61, 119
Holos Project Earth, 96
Holy Spirit, 15
hope, 40, 65, 89
Houston, Jean, 5n, 24–25, 98
human consciousness, *see* Consciousness
Hutson, Harry, ix, 65
Huxley, Aldous, 10
inclusive, xxxv, 30, 46, 59, 81, 91
Ingerman, Sandra, 79, 122
Institute of Noetic Sciences (IONS), 3, 24n, 55n, 96–97, 102
intelligence, xx, xxxvi, 8, 62, 91, 110
"Interactions of Two Persons", 28
intuitive, xxix–xxx, xxxiii, xxxiv, 13, 20, 38, 44, 78, 82, 85, 110
Isbey, Jo Anne, 54n
Jung, Carl G., xxx, xxxi, 2, 15, 18, 25–26, 46, 50, 123
Kaufman, Scott Barry, 18
Kaufman, Stuart, 23
Kelly, Kevin, 93
Kelly, Sean, 60
Kilmann, Ralph, 70–71
Kofman, Fred, 39, 62n
Kripal, Jeffrey J., 20–21, 83–84, 105–106, 119

Kuhn, Thomas, 107
Kumar, Raj, 13
Laszlo, Chris, 38, 40, 67, 86n, 95n
Laszlo, Ervin, 62, 115, 122
leadership, xv, 33, 35–41 *passim*, 50, 60, 108–109
   developing creative choices and social purpose, 35, 38
   inner experience and outer behavior, 35–36
   inspiring others to a higher purpose, 35, 39–40
   integrating the rational and the transrational, 35, 37
   transcendent, 39–40
   with soul, 38
Lemmens, Pieter, 93–94
limen, xxxiv
liminal,
   actions, 23–27, 119
   being intentional, 11, 17–18
   consciousness, *see* consciousness
   experiences, xxxiv–xxxv, 11, 14–19, 24, 26, 72, 74, 77, 119
   formation, 12, 17
   groups (L-groups), 47–48, 72, 107, 119
   human interaction, 23, 28–30
   leaders, 35–41, 119
   methods, 65, 67–80, 119
   narrative, 106–108
   need for, xxxvii, 108
   self, 1, 2, 19–21, 23–32, 77, 86, 111, 119, 120
   spaces, xxxiv, 17, 29, 48, 68, 75, 107, 120, 127
   state, xxii, xxiii, xxix (n), xxxiv, 2, 28, 47, 55, 78
   unintentional experiences, 11, 14–17
liminal teams, 46, 49–51
   comparison to hi-performing teams, 49–51
   organic flow of, 50
   power of eight, 44
   synchronized and aligned, 50
liminality, xxix, xxxiv–xxxv, 11–14, 48, 53, 55, 62
   obstacles to, 48
Lincoln, Abraham, 18
Lorimer, David, xxxiv (n), 62n, 99, 109
love, 27, 31, 55, 60, 85, 87, 97, 107, 111, 125
   in organizations, 120
   invisible strong force of attraction, 60
   serotonin, dopamine, oxycontin, 60n
   the urge to merge, 60
   verb, packed with action, 60, 120
Maheshwari, Anil K., 57–58
managers, xxxv, 31, 34, 49, 58, 65, 68–69
Manifest Nirvana, 97
Marshall, Perry, 78, 107n
Maslow, Abraham H., 59
materialist worldview, xix, xxxiii, xxxvii, 3, 33, 70, 85, 99, 110, 120
McTaggart, Lynne, 43–44
meditation, xxi, xxix, xxxiii, 8, 11, 13, 16, 18, 38, 67, 68, 71, 121
Merton, Thomas, 16–17
Mind-at-Large, 10
mindful universe, xxxviii, 1
mindfulness, xxxiii, 56–57, 67–68, 71, 101
monkey minds, 24
moral consciousness, 57, 76

Mossbridge, Julia, 70
Motl, James, 15
music, xxix, 11, 14, 17, 38, 77–78, 105, 121
mystical,
　experiences, xxxiii, xxxviii, 6, 10, 15, 19–20, 78, 110, 120, 126–127
　paths, 90n, xxxvi
near-death experiences (NDEs), 4, 140
Nirvana, 19, 45n
noetic, 2, 55–56, 96
　experiences, 2
non-duality, xxxvi, 5, 82n, 86, 106, 120, 127
non-local consciousness, xxii, xxx, xxxiii, xxxvi, 4–5, 9, 109, 120
non-physical teachers, 25–26
noosphere, 33, 93–94, 102, 120
NTL Institute of Applied Behavioral Science, 65n, 71, 141
numinous, 47, 121
One Mountain, Many Paths, 97
organization development (OD), xxx, 30, 55, 68–71, 115
organizations, xv, xxi, xxix–xxxi, xxxv, 9, 30, 32, 34, 38, 43, 48, 53–63 *passim*, 68–80 *passim*, 108, 115, 117, 122, 123
　archetype, 56
　higher purpose, 35, 53, 60, 61
　love in, 120
　spirit, 38, 43, 53–54, 56, 61–62
　total interconnectedness, 53, 56–59, 123
　transcendence, 54–56, 60, 62, 123
Pavlovich, Kathryn, 71

perennial spiritual wisdom, 5, 121
Perspectiva, 93, 100
Philemon, 25
physicalism, 4, 121
Planck, Max, 107
polarities, 46n, 48, 60, 82–83, 85, 106
portals to Consciousness, xxix, 11, 17, 76, 105, 121
post-materialism, 70, 99, 105, 108, 121
Potter, Harry, 14–15
power of eight, *see* liminal teams
presence, xxxv, 5, 10, 15, 20, 47, 69, 91–92, 121
prism, 7, 121
psyche, 15, 25–26, 37, 100, 118, 121
psychedelic drugs, 12
quantum biology, 4–5, 105, 121
Ramamoorthy, Sandarasubramanyan, 45
Ransford, Emmanuel, 8
rational self, 28–31, 121
reality, xvi–xix, xxxiii, xxxviii, 1, 3–10 *passim*, 82, 85–86, 96, 105–106, 110, 118–122 *passim*, 127–128
Renesch, John, 56, 117
Robinson, John, 15
Rowling, J.K., 14
Rowson, Jonathan, 93, 100
Rubin, Rick, 77
Russ, Helen, 55–56
sacred sites, 15, 76
Schwantes, Marcel, 60, 120
Science and Nonduality (SAND), 101
Scientific and Medical Network (SMN), xxxiv (n), 3, 99, 102

self, 17, 19–21, 23–32 *passim*, 38, 62, 69, 77, 92, 100, 111, 115, 120, 121, 122, 125–126
self-actualization, 39, 59, 78, 122
self-awareness, xxix, 9, 30, 37, 56, 85, 117, 125–126
self-transcendence, 56n, 110, 122
Senge, Peter M., 91–92, 121
Sexton, Terence, 74–75, 85n, 89
shadow, xxxvii, 122
shamanic journeys, 79, 122
Shapiro, Rabbi Rami, v, xxv, xxxvii, 113
Shift Network, xxxvii (n), 98
showing up in organizations, 23, 30–32
simple rules, 109–111, 122
    develop intuitive practices, 110
    develop transformative relationships, 110–111
    learn more about non-material reality, 110
skunk works, 79–80
Smitsman, Anneloes, vi, 5n, 24–25, 39, 98, 109n
Snow, Shane, 49
social polarizations, xxx, xxxvii, 83, 85
spacetime, 7, 12, 20
spirit in organizations, 53–54, 122
spirituality, xvi, xxi, xxxiv, 5, 13, 15, 25, 38, 53–54, 58, 61, 67, 79, 86, 105, 115
    spiritual coaches, 68, 73–74, 97
    spiritual development, 38
    spiritual partnership, 28–29, 80, 102
spontaneous guidance from the universe, 62, 115, 122

Srikantia, Param, 33n, 89n
Stein, Murray, 2, 46n
stories, 1, 17, 75–77, 85, 91, 106
subjective reality, 2, 3–10, 20
Sullwold, Edith, 43
superposition, 4, 7
Swimme, Brian, 60
symbols, 17, 21, 24, 46, 68, 73, 75–77, 84, 115
synchronicity, 13, 16, 50, 72, 73, 86, 102, 122, 127
systemic climate collapse, 93
teams, 43–51
    hold tension, 43, 45–46
    intention, 43–45
    patience, 43, 46–47
technosphere, 93, 122
Teilhard de Chardin, Pierre, 31–32, 120
thin place, 123
total interconnectedness, 56–59, 123
training groups (T-groups), 48, 68, 71–73
TRANS4M Centre for Integral Development, 100
transcend differences, 65, 66, 81–87
transcendent, 4, 59, 101, 107, 109, 121, 123
    experiences, xxxviii, 14
    function, 46, 48, 50, 123
    leaders, 39–40
    organization, 54–57, 59–62, 123
    practices, 33–34
    reality, 12, 20, 86
    thinking, xxxv
transformation, xv, xvii, 19, 32, 60, 68, 79, 90n, 97–98, 101, 123
transpersonal, xxxvi, 80, 123

transrational, 37, 123
Tsao, Frederick Chavalit, 34n, 37n, 40, 67, 101n
Tuesday cone, 26
tunneling, 5, 7, 102, 123
Universal Consciousness, Universal Mind, Cosmic Consciousness, xxii, 3, 7n, 117, 123
use of self, 69
Vaill, Peter B., 33n, 36n, 38, 49n, 61
Vedic wisdom, 57–58
Warwick, Clifford, 9–10
Wheatley, Margaret, 38
white fragility, 84
wholeness, xxx, 24, 25, 37, 40, 53, 82, 85, 89–103, 108, 115, 119, 124, 127
 narrative, 94–95
 of the Earth, 92–93
Wilbur, Ken, 81
Williams, Ben, 6n, 11n
wisdom, xx–xxiii, xxxi, 5, 6, 27, 48, 57, 62, 76, 86, 90, 93, 96, 98, 105, 110, 116, 121, 122
Wizard of Oz, 19
Woollacott, Marjorie Hines, 11n, 16
world soul, xxxi
Worthen, Molly, 74
Yunkaporta, Tyson, 44
Zen, 32
Zukav, Gary, xxxiv (n), 25, 27n, 29, 105n
Zweig, Connie, xxxvi (n), 27, 102

Acknowledgements

I am indebted to the many scientists, philosophers, and theologians who have wrestled with the "Hard Problem of Consciousness" and its implications for our future. I have only cited a few in this book but know that there is an extensive literature that is continuing to grow.

I am grateful for my family, friends, and colleagues who provided invaluable feedback on my early drafts. They are Curt Ackley, Gregory Blann, Gervase Bushe, Michael Ciszewski, Tom Cockley, Dianne Collins, Kate Cowie, Argentine Craig, Charles Fox, Shane Hadden, Deborah Holbrook, Ron Johnson, John Nkun, Eric Olson, Judith Olson, Loren Olson, Sankar Ramamoorthy, Nanette Smith, Anneloes Smitsman, and Peter Veronesi.

I am especially indebted to Kate Cowie for her encouragement throughout the process and to Ted Tschudy and Harry Hutson, Jr. who offered their valuable critiques and insights on behalf of the NTL Institute. I am greatly honored that Dianne Collins took time from her busy schedule to write the Foreword.

I also must acknowledge the writing assistance from Google's Bard and Chat GPT-4, while asserting that the content in the book is from my memory and experience, my dreams, Consciousness, and the sources I identify in the footnotes.

Without the work of the organizations and associations that are working to bring the paradigm/worldview of Consciousness to public awareness, this book could not have been written. In Chapter 9 I have acknowledged those I know about and have learned from during the past several years.

These organizations and others continue to push the boundaries of what we know about Consciousness with empirical studies of consciousness, neural networks, near-death experiences, and the function of the brain, heart, and gut. I believe my grandchildren and future great-grandchildren and everyone and everything on the planet will benefit from their work.

I dedicate this book to Judith who has given her love and support that created the conditions that enabled my writing.

Edwin E. Olson

May 20, 2023

https://www.wholenessconsciousness.com/

About the Author

Ed Olson was a survey research director for National Analysts, Inc., and senior associate at the Institute for the Advancement of Medical Communication. He then was appointed as professor of information service at the University of Maryland, College Park, and then professor of management at Baldwin-Wallace College. He finished his full-time professional career as an organization development and diversity consultant to many companies and government agencies.

He is a member of the NTL Institute of Applied Behavioral Science and a National Certified Counselor. Currently he teaches online MBA courses for the University of Maryland, Global Campus (UMGC), and leads workshops for the Uplands Lifelong Learning Institute (ULLI), the NTL Institute of Applied Behavioral Science, and the Chautauqua Institution (New York). He applies the theories and methods of the sciences of complexity, consciousness, quantum, applied behavioral science, and spirituality to the study of human, organization, and societal development.

Ed has a BA in Philosophy (St. Olaf College); MS in Pastoral Counseling (Loyola College); MA and PhD in Government (American University); and is a graduate of the Science for Ministry Program, Princeton Theological Seminary.

He is the author of *Become Conscious of Wholeness: Humanity's Only Future* (2021, Resource Publications); *And God Created Wholeness: A*

Spirituality of Catholicity (2018, Orbis Books); *Finding Reality: Four Ways of Knowing* (2014, Archway Publications); *Keep the Bathwater: Emergence of the Sacred in Science and Religion* (2009, Island Sound Press); *Facilitating Organization Change: Lessons from Complexity Science* (2001, Jossey-Bass/Wiley), and numerous papers and presentations at national and international conferences.

Ed is married to Judith. They have four children (James, Eric, Loren, and Amy) and eight grandchildren (Preston, Arne, Arlo, Greta, Zeida, Tuesday, Cisco, and Clover).

https://www.wholenessconsciousness.com/

www.ingramcontent.com/pod-product-compliance
Lightning Source LLC
LaVergne TN
LVHW051216070526
838200LV00063B/4922